GOD'S
UNCONDITIONAL
LOVE

by
Bill Freeman

MINISTRY
PUBLICATIONS
Scottsdale, Arizona

First Edition 1994
Second Edition 2000

Library of Congress Catalog
Card Number: 98-68164

ISBN 0-914271-96-2

Ministry Publications

PO Box 48255
Spokane, WA 99228
(509) 466-4777 / (800) 573-4105
Email: ministry@thechristian.org
www.thechristian.org

Printed in the United States of America

Contents

Preface

This volume comprises spoken messages given in the Spring of 1989 in Scottsdale, Arizona. The main burden of these messages is focused on the way God's love reaches us in whatever condition we may find ourselves.

God's love is revealed in many different ways throughout the Bible, but the *unconditional* nature of His love is uniquely unveiled in the Old Testament book of Hosea. Here we see unconditional love portrayed in God telling Hosea to marry a harlot (Hosea 1:2) and then to continue to love her while she is unfaithful (Hosea 3:1). This is a vivid picture of the nature of God's unconditional love — it works over any kind of failure or sinful condition.

In the New Testament the unconditional nature of God's love is detailed by the apostle Paul in Romans 8:35-39 when he declares to the universe that *nothing* is able to separate us from God's unconditional love. No outward problem, no inward condition, no environmental dealing, no opposition, no person, no demonic force can separate us from the love of God which is in Christ Jesus our Lord!

God's Unconditional Love is published with the expectation that the reading of this book will strengthen the revelation that, even in the midst of the most extreme situations, God's unconditional love reaches us.

— *Bill Freeman*
August 2000

S cripture quotations are taken from a combination of translations including *The New King James Version,*[†] *The King James Version, The New American Standard Version,*[§] etc. Minor changes have been made in the various versions from time to time to give a better rendering of the Hebrew and Greek texts.

Throughout the Scripture quotations, words are italicized for added emphasis.

[†] Scripture taken from the New King James Version. Copyright © 1982 by Thomas Nelson, Inc. Used by permission. All rights reserved.

[§] "Scripture taken from the NEW AMERICAN STANDARD BIBLE, © 1960, 1962, 1963, 1968, 1971, 1972, 1973, 1975, 1977, by the Lockman Foundation. Used by permission."

"Then the LORD said to me, Go again, love a woman who is loved by a lover and is committing adultery, *just like* the love of the LORD for the children of Israel...."

❦ *Hosea 3:1*

"For I am persuaded that neither death nor life, nor angels nor principalities nor powers, nor things present nor things to come, nor height nor depth, nor any other created thing, shall be able to separate us from the love of God which is in Christ Jesus our Lord."

❦ *Romans 8:38-39*

1

The Revelation of God's Unconditional Love

To speak of God's unconditional love is to utter a wonderful fact about God's nature. He loves because He *chooses* to love and for no other reason. His love is not dependent upon finding something in us that merits His love. His love is without conditions — it is *un*conditional. This kind of love is expressed in the Lord's words to Israel: [7] "The LORD did not set His love on you nor choose you because you were more in number than any other people, for you were the least of all peoples; [8] but because the LORD loves you ..." (Deut. 7:7-8). In other words, God loves because He chooses to love, not because of a *reason* found outside of Himself.

God's unconditional love is revealed throughout the Old and New Testaments, but in no other book in the Bible do we see the unconditional nature of His love as in Hosea. When we touch this book, we sense that we are treading ground that we have never trod before. We see God's unconditional love coming to the least likely object of love — an object that does not, by any human standard, merit or deserve love. As we look into the book of Hosea, may the Lord by His Spirit give us a fresh revelation of the breadth, length, height, and depth of God's unconditional love (Eph. 3:18-19).

The effect of the revelation

Let us consider how the revelation of God's unconditional love affects us. First, it affects our relationship to the Lord. Knowing His love, even understanding what God's unconditional love is, will have a tremendous effect on how we relate to the Lord day by day. Second, God's unconditional love also affects how I relate to myself. It affects how I feel about myself and how I understand myself in light of my relationship with God. Third, understanding and enjoying this realm of God's unconditional love greatly affects our relationships with one another in the Body of Christ. Fourth, it affects our relationship to humanity — to fallen man, to those who are lost. And fifth, God's unconditional love affects our relationship to His eternal purpose. God's love toward us always has a goal in view, and that goal is absolutely related to His purpose being worked out in this universe. So we see that God's unconditional love affects all these areas — my relationship with God, with myself, with the saints, with every human being, and with God's eternal purpose.

On the other hand, if we lack the revelation of God's love toward us, it will also affect all these areas. We may have known the Lord for twenty or thirty years and still not know the extent of God's love toward us. Zephaniah 3:17 says, "The LORD your God in your midst, the Mighty One, will save; He will rejoice over you with gladness, He will quiet [or, rest] you in His love, He will rejoice over you with singing." God wants to quiet us and rest us in His unconditional love. Our resting place is the love of God.

The demonstration of God's unconditional love

To apprehend the unconditional love of God, we need to see it demonstrated in the book of Hosea. The only way to describe this love is to look into the Word and see God's own utterances about His relationship to His people. We can look at the book of Hosea in two ways: first, look at the condition of the ones that God's love is directed toward; second, look at the nature of the unconditional love of God toward the ones He is loving, especially in light of their condition.

Hosea 1:2-3 says, ² "When the LORD began to speak by Hosea, the LORD said to Hosea: Go, take yourself a wife of harlotry and children of harlotry, for the land has committed great harlotry by departing from the LORD. ³ So he went and took Gomer the daughter of Diblaim, and she conceived and bore him a son." God uses Hosea's relationship with Gomer to demonstrate His relationship with His people. By telling Hosea, a righteous, godly man who was the Lord's prophet, to take a wife of whoredoms, or harlotry, God is depicting the nature of His love toward us. He tells Hosea to take a woman of harlotry to be his wife. Then He interprets the deeper significance of this act by saying, "for the land has committed great harlotry by departing from the LORD." Thus, God wants us to understand through His Word that just as Hosea took a wife to himself in her vile condition, so God takes His people to Himself in their vile condition. Hosea's act demonstrates and reveals the nature of God's unconditional love toward us.

Gomer, the name of the woman Hosea was to take as a wife, reveals the depths of the nature of God's unconditional love. *Gomer* is derived from the Hebrew word *gamar* which means "cease, come to an end, fail." In other words, God was telling Hosea, "Go take *failure* to be your wife," or "Go take *that which has come to an end* to be your wife." This shows the nature of God's love toward us. He loves us when we have no potential, no victory, when we have come to an end — when we are nothing but failure. The name *Gomer* not only means "failure," but it also has the meaning of "completion" or "perfection." So this woman was complete or perfected in her failure. She was a harlot. She filled up the measure of harlotry to the uttermost. She committed not merely one transgression but multiple transgressions. She reached a state of completion and is ironically spoken of as being perfected in harlotry. She was that low, that base. She was perfected in her harlotry because she was fully experienced in sinning and in rebellion. She was fully developed, perfected, and completed in the realm of failure. She was not partially a failure, but she was a total failure.

Gomer was the daughter of *Diblaim,* whose name in Hebrew means "dried, rotten, corrupted figs." So Hosea was to marry a failure, a woman perfected in her sins, in harlotry, whose mother's name means "corruption" and "rottenness." These verses at the very beginning of the book of Hosea depict the nature of God's love toward us.

God tells Hosea to take Gomer, this "wife of harlotry," to be his wife. Later in chapter 3, God tells him to love her. First

He says *take;* then He says *love* this woman. This demonstrates the Lord's love toward us. He takes us and then lavishes His love on us despite our failed condition.

This Old Testament description of Gomer has a New Testament counterpart. Ephesians 2:1-3 says, [1] "And you He made alive, who were dead in trespasses and sins, [2] in which you once walked according to the course of this world, according to the prince of the power of the air, the spirit who now works in the sons of disobedience, [3] among whom also we all once conducted ourselves in the lusts of our flesh, fulfilling the desires of the flesh and of the mind, and were by nature children of wrath, just as the others." These verses describe us as failures, perfected in sinning, rotten and corrupted, living under the dominion of the devil, living out the drives of the flesh, and being by nature children of wrath, even as the rest of mankind. This is the New Testament description of Gomer.

Then verses 4-5 say, [4] "But God, who is rich in mercy, because of His great love with which He loved us, [5] even when we were dead in trespasses..." Even when we were in that situation, God loved us. Here again is God loving people who are failures, perfected in their failure, and who are spoiled and corrupted to the uttermost. And verses 5-6 show God demonstrating His love: [5] "[He] made us alive together with Christ (by grace you have been saved), [6] and raised us up together, and made us sit together in the heavenlies in Christ Jesus." This unveils the nature of God's love toward us.

We usually live in the realm or on the level of *our* worthiness and *our* condition. In this realm, whether or not God loves us depends very much upon whether or not *we* feel we are lovable. If we feel that we have "measured up" a little bit — that we have had a "better" week or have done a few extra good things — then we feel that we can receive the love of God. Many times our perception of God's attitude toward us is based on our own feelings about ourself. But in Hosea, the Lord presents the example of Gomer, who is the absolute totality of failure, the perfection of harlotry, with a mother whose name means *corruption* and *rottenness*. Then He tells Hosea to take her in marriage. This shows that though God's people have departed from Him, they are still the objects of His unconditional love. From this we see that God's love is far beyond our human concept or idea.

Alluring love

In Hosea chapter 2 the Lord continues to describe this woman who symbolizes God's people. In verse 13 He says, "...the days of the Baals to which she burned incense. She decked herself with her earrings and jewelry, and went after her lovers. Then she forgot Me, says the Lord." She totally forgot the Lord and went after her lovers. We would think the Lord would then respond, "Therefore, behold, I will strike her in judgment." But He does not say that. He says, "Therefore, behold, I will allure her, will bring her into the wilderness, and speak comfort to her" (v. 14). "I will speak comfort to her" literally means "I will speak to her heart." So here in Hosea, the Lord describes His people who went after other lovers — even other gods, Baals — and completely forgot the Lord. Yet the nature of God's love toward His people is such that, even in this state, when she has forgotten Him and has gone to idolatry, He will bring her into the wilderness. In other words, He will bring her into an environment, into a circumstance, that causes her to feel her need. In that kind of situation, He will attract her, allure her, and seek to win her.

This is God's love toward the objects of His love. And the objects of His love are simply those whom He has chosen to love. In Romans 9:13 the Lord says, "Jacob I have loved, but Esau I have hated." Jacob was the object of God's love regardless of his condition — regardless of his rebellion, his conniving, his deceiving. Despite all that, the Lord followed him as "the hound of heaven." Wherever Jacob went, the Lord was there alluring him, seeking him, winning him. This is another example of God's love toward His people, and it is absolutely an unconditional kind of love. In the same way, in the book of Hosea there are no conditions to meet in order to receive God's love. Gomer, symbolizing God's people, has forgotten the Lord. She has gone to idols. Because this is her state, the Lord says that He will bring her into the wilderness and speak to her heart tenderly. He will do these things in order to allure and win her.

Covenant love

Then in Hosea 2:19-20 the Lord says, [19] "I will betroth you to Me forever; yes, I will betroth you to Me in righteousness and justice [or, judgment], in lovingkindness and mercy; [20] I will betroth you to Me in faithfulness, and you shall know the

LORD." Here again, though His people are in a rebellious condition, the Lord says, "I will betroth you to Me forever." This definitely tells us that He has plans for them — plans for a future marriage and union with Him. He is going to betroth; He is going to enter into a contract, a pledge, like a covenant, to love and to win them. So again in chapter 2 we see the nature of God's love. Each time His love is revealed, it is revealed toward ones in a rebellious condition, a fallen condition, a sinful condition — conditions that merit absolutely nothing, that deserve nothing but judgment and hell. But all the while, God keeps coming and revealing His love in an unconditional way.

The meaning of "unconditional" love

Hosea 3:1 says, "Then the LORD said to me, Go again, love a woman who is loved by a lover." "Loved by a lover" may be translated "loved by a husband." This indicates that Hosea, the husband-lover, loved his wife, Gomer, who was committing adultery. So he took this wife of harlotry, and she bore children to him and then continued in that same kind of harlot living. This can be likened to your becoming a believer and knowing the Lord for a period of time, and then turning away from Him and going back to your old lifestyle, or manner of life, and committing spiritual adultery with many other things. Let me say to you categorically that God's love to you is *still* unconditional because you are the object of His love. It is eternal love based upon an eternal choice and can never be destroyed or eradicated.

So, in a sense, we are the victims of God's love. We are the objects of God's love. The Lord tells Hosea, "Go again, love a woman who is loved by a husband and is committing adultery, *just like* the love of the LORD for the children of Israel." These two words, "just like," are the key words that reveal the nature of God's unconditional love. Humanly speaking, that woman did not deserve a thing but to be cast off. Yet God says to love that woman "*just like* the love of the LORD for the children of Israel."

This is what the love of the Lord is like. This is how God loves you and how God loves me. There have been times I have awakened in the morning thinking about my spiritual condition and how I am doing. I have found myself basing my relationship with the Lord and His love toward me on my condition. But when God's unconditional love, revealed in the book of Hosea, was opened up to me, everything changed. It is absolutely a reality that we can rest in His love (Zeph. 3:17).

At the end of Hosea 3:1, the Lord gives more description of the condition of His people: "who look to other gods and love the raisin cakes of the pagans." This indicates that the children of Israel were fully distracted in idolatry, addicted to idolatry. Ephraim is spoken of in this way. An idol is anything that replaces God and usurps God in our life. It does not have to be a statue of Buddha. It can be an automobile. It can be a bank account. It can be a person, a relationship. It can be watching television. It can be whatever gives us pleasure in our flesh. It may give us pleasure, but it can actually be idolatry, as Colossians 3:5 says: "covetousness, which is idolatry." Covetousness refers to having inordinate, sinful, pleasurable desires that are directed toward some object. This is idolatry.

Ephraim was joined to idols, and at one point the Lord said, "let him alone" (Hosea 4:17). Here God leaves His people to themselves in order that they would become disgusted with themselves. Then Ephraim came under the allurement and the attraction of the love of God. So at the end of the book of Hosea, the Lord declares that after Ephraim observes Him and hears Him and enjoys His love, he shall say, "What have I to do anymore with idols?" (14:8). In other words, Ephraim has become enthralled with God's love. Once he was addicted to idolatry, but now he has been totally captured by God's love. So he just drops the idols. This is yet another picture of the nature of God's unconditional love.

Dependable love

Now let us look at Hosea 6:1-3: [1] "Come, and let us return to the LORD; for He has torn, but He will heal us; He has stricken, but He will bind us up. [2] After two days He will revive us; on the third day He will raise us up, that we may live in His sight. [3] Let us know, let us pursue the knowledge of the LORD. His going forth is established as the morning; He will come to us like the rain, like the latter and former rain to the earth." Here we see that, on one hand, God's love takes the form of tearing and striking; on the other hand, His love takes the form of binding us up, healing us, and raising us up. Both forms of His love are necessary for us to "live in His sight."

Verse 3 says that the Lord's going forth is established as the morning. That means His love is absolutely dependable. It is established as the morning. In this universe, you can depend upon tomorrow morning. You can depend upon the fact that there will be another morning. How dependable the morning is! And toward you — in your idolatry, in your failure, in your rottenness, in your corruption, in the filling up of your sins — His love is as dependable as the morning. This is God's love. This is unconditional love.

You can count on the fact that God loves you, not because your condition merits His love, but rather because God's love issues out of Himself, unrelated to our condition. Ephesians 1:4 says, "He chose us in Him before the foundation of the world." And verse 5 tells us that His choosing us was "according to the good pleasure of His will." Thus, out of His own good pleasure, He chose us. He selected us. It did not make any difference what our condition was. As those selected and chosen, we have become the very objects of God's love. And this love is dependable; it is eternal, everlasting. Praise the Lord for the nature of God's love!

Gentle love

Now let us look at another example of God's unconditional love in Hosea 11:1-4. In verse 1 the Lord declares, "When Israel was a child, I loved him, and out of Egypt I called My son." This verse has a double application: to Israel in their formative years, and to the Lord Jesus in the early years of His life on the earth (Matt. 2:15). In relation to Israel verse 2 says, "As they [the prophets] called them [Israel], so they went from them; they sacrificed to the Baals, and burned incense to carved images." In other words, Israel's sin was not just a little mistake. They purposely sacrificed to other gods, and actually burned incense to carved images. The very ones who knew the living God ran after other loves. They were filled with idolatry and addicted to it.

Then in verses 3-4 the Lord says, [3] "I taught Ephraim to walk, taking them by their arms; but they did not know that I healed them. [4] I drew them with gentle cords, with bands of love." "Gentle cords" can also be translated "cords of a man." The Lord drew His people with cords of a man, not cords of a beast. They are not the kind of cords that you pull beasts with, but gentle cords. He does not treat us like a beast but tenderly comes with gentle cords, "with bands of love."

Then in verse 4 the Lord continues, "And I was to them as those who take the yoke from their neck. I stooped and fed them." This means God's love is a stooping love. God's love comes down to where we are. And when we are under a yoke, He removes it. Yet because we have been under a yoke so long, we do not know how to behave without one. We have been in bondage for so long that, when He removes the yoke, we cannot get up by ourselves. So He not only removes the yoke, but He also comes down to where we are and stoops to feed us. Praise the Lord!

This means that the Lord meets you exactly where you are. The nature of His love does not require that you first come up to a certain level. But just as you are, the way you are, God will come down to you and stoop and feed you. Praise the Lord for this kind of love. This is the gentle nature of God's unconditional love revealed to us in Hosea.

Intrinsic love

Hosea 11:7 says, "My people are bent on backsliding from Me. Though they call to the Most High, none at all exalt Him." This describes a kind of religious profession that has no heart in it. It is like a person going through the motions of religion, but who in reality is bent on backsliding. This condition is well-described in the lines of a hymn: "Prone to wander, Lord, I feel it, prone to leave the God I love."

Often we come to a point where we feel, "God can't love me anymore. I've passed the point of no return. He might be able to love others, but not me." This is what happened to John Bunyan, the author of *Pilgrim's Progress*. For seven years he was under the tyranny of his own thoughts and of the devil; both were telling him that he had committed the unpardonable sin and had gone beyond the love and grace of God. He was tormented for those years. This happens to us in our experience, especially when we have continual failures, when it happens again and again and we seem to be bent on backsliding.

Let us just stop ourselves where we are. Do not analyze yourself or imagine that God's love for you is based on your own feelings. Instead, look at the Word. Listen to the Lord's reaction to those who are prone to wander, who are addicted to backsliding, who have, so to speak, filled up the measure of their sins in whatever area. In Hosea 11:7 we see Israel bent on backsliding. Then the Lord says in verse 8, "How can I give you up, Ephraim? How can I hand you over, Israel? How can I make you like Admah? How can I set you like Zeboiim?" In Deuteronomy 29:23 Admah and Zeboiim are grouped together with Sodom and Gomorrah. When God gave up Sodom and Gomorrah and destroyed them, He did the same with Admah and Zeboiim. So here He says to Ephraim, "How can I make you like Admah? How can I set you like Zeboiim? My heart churns within Me." This is God.

This shows us that the nature of God's unconditional love is intrinsic to God Himself. That means it is organically a part of Him. Have you ever had compassion toward someone? You felt mercy toward them. It was in you intrinsically. You loved, you wept, you went out to them. It came right out of you because it was what was in you. God said, "My heart churns within Me." This shows that God's love toward us is not a doctrine to Him. It is intrinsic to His being. It belongs to His nature. It is the way He reacts, the way He feels. Even with Israel in a backslidden condition He says, [8] "My heart churns within Me; My sympathy [compassion] is stirred. [9] I will not execute the fierceness of My anger; I will not again destroy Ephraim. For I am God, and not man" (Hosea 11:8-9). Praise the Lord, our God feels this way.

Uncompelled love

In Hosea 14:4-8 the Lord says, [4] "I will heal their backsliding, I will love them freely, for My anger has turned away from him. [5] I will be like the dew to Israel; he shall grow like the lily, and lengthen his roots like Lebanon. [6] His branches shall spread; his beauty shall be like an olive tree, and his fragrance like Lebanon. [7] Those who dwell under his shadow shall return; they shall be revived like grain, and grow like the vine. Their scent shall be like the wine of Lebanon. [8] Ephraim shall say, 'What have I to do anymore with idols?' I have heard and observed him. I am like a green cypress tree; your fruit is found in Me." These verses show us that God's unconditional love is dependable, gentle, and intrinsic. In verse 4 He says, "I will love them freely." The Hebrew word for "freely" means uncompelled. No one has to compel God to love him. Inwardly, voluntarily, freely, without any compelling, He loves us. This is the nature of God's love toward us. So in the book of Hosea we see a revelation of God's unconditional love.

Practical love

Practically, how does God's love affect my experience? How does it affect the way I relate to the Lord, to myself, to the brothers and sisters, and to other people? Having a revelation of the nature of the love of God will change our relationships in each of these areas. We are persons with the love of God "poured out in our hearts by the Holy Spirit who was given to us" (Rom. 5:5). This love is demonstrated and manifested in our very being to be enjoyed by us and others. This is the nature of God's love. And our relationship with the Lord is based upon our resting in this love. In John 15:9 the Lord said, "As the Father loved Me, I also have loved you; abide in My love." Just rest in His love; just stay in His love.

The book of Hosea reveals God's love to His people in the midst of a dark background, in a most despicable kind of condition. God illustrates His love toward Israel by telling Hosea to take a wife of harlotry and then to love her even though she continues in her adultery. This is the nature of God's love. We also need to be persons who are under this influence and this allurement. We just need to allow the Lord to draw us with gentle cords, with bands of love, that our hearts may be touched.

This unconditional love of God was demonstrated to us through Christ's death on the cross. Romans 5:8 says, *"while we were yet sinners, Christ died for us."* And Romans 5:6 says, "Christ died for the ungodly." Then in verse 7 Paul says that someone might "dare to die" for a good man. But God did not die for a good man. Instead, *"while* we were *yet sinners*, Christ died for us." So this is a demonstration of the love of God.

Ephesians 5:25 says that Christ "loved the church and gave Himself up for her." He loved the church not because the church at that time was intrinsically beautiful. She had no beauty. We were like the rotten figs that Hosea describes. We were failures, ungodly, sinful, rebellious, and addicted to idolatry. In New Testament terms this kind of love is described in Ephesians 2:4-5: [4] "But God, who is rich in mercy, because of His great love with which He loved us, [5] even when we were dead in trespasses, made us alive together with Christ." This is God's unconditional love. God's love is in this dimension. So now our hearts simply need to be opened up to this revelation.

We should not presume that we really know God's character and love. We may have had a difficult childhood, being handled abusively, and now we may project our parents' ways of relating to us onto God. In other words, we think that is the way God is. But we have to realize God is God. He says, "I am God, and not man" (Hosea 11:9). He is not your natural father or mother. We need to have a revelation of how God loves us.

Now we just need to come to Him. Just as we are, come to Him. Have you failed? Then you are a candidate to come to Him. He will take you to Himself. Are you rotten? You also are a candidate for God's love. Do you feel corrupted and spoiled? Maybe your humanity has become spoiled. You have sinned yourself out — you feel wasted. Do you realize that God's love to you is not based upon any beauty or potential in you? It is just His nature, intrinsically, to love you, the object of His love. He cannot help Himself. He cannot help but love us.

We all need to shout, Hallelujah! We are all objects of God's unconditional love. Let Him bring you into the wilderness, attract you, and speak to you. Let Him woo your heart simply to love Him. It is not a matter of someone coercing or forcing you to break away from the idols you are joined to. It is a matter of just enjoying the love of God in Christ Jesus our Lord, from which nothing can separate you. This love will cause you to say, "What have I to do anymore with idols?"

Oh, may the Lord attract us all as we see this love of God that wins our hearts. Let Him come down and meet you where you are. Let Him stoop and feed you. He does not expect you to even lift up your head. He will take away the yoke and He will come down just where you are. If you can only say, "O Lord" — if that is all you can get out because that is just where you are — then that is where He loves you. He loves you right where you are, just as you are. No wonder we sing, "Just as I am, without one plea, but that Thy blood was shed for me."

God's love has been demonstrated. This is the nature of God's love revealed in Hosea; and this love affects our relationship with Him, with ourself, with one another, and with His purpose. This love causes us to shout with Paul to the whole universe that nothing "shall be able to separate us from the love of God which is in Christ Jesus our Lord" (Rom. 8:39).

Spend some time before the Lord, fellowshipping with Him in your heart. Just enjoy His intrinsic, covenant love. Let His unconditional love gently allure you in whatever condition you find yourself. Be certain that His love is dependable as the morning. Let the effects of this love reach into every area of your being and into all your relationships.

2

The Objects of
God's Unconditional Love

The kind of love God has for us

The book of Hosea opens up to us a revelation of God's love in its unconditional sense. In this Old Testament book we see God's love toward us according to God's definition and thought, not according to our thought and limited view. At the same time, Hosea unveils something of the very character and nature of God. We have probably never fathomed the kind of love God has toward us. Indeed, the example of Hosea's relationship with his wife Gomer may cause us to shake our head in disbelief. Yet that very relationship is a picture of God's relationship with us and the kind of love He has toward us.

God's unfathomable love is toward fallen, sinful man, who, in his degraded condition, is described as "a mass of corruption" (the meaning of "Diblaim" in Hosea 1:3). In the New Testament book of Romans we again see this same love that goes beyond our human thought. As we mentioned in chapter 1, Romans 5:6-8 tells us that God demonstrated His love to us by dying for us *while* we were in a state of being ungodly, when there was no improvement, no bettering of our condition.

In the same sense, *while* Gomer is a harlot, *while* she is a failure and a mass of corruption, *while* she is a spoiled piece of humanity — *while* she is in this state — Hosea is to take her and to love her, and to continue to love her. May this kind of word sink into our inner being, be indelibly etched upon our insides, and stay with us for life. God's love is of this nature. It is not according to our fickle ideas or our conditional concepts. We cannot interpret whether or not He loves us based on our own subjective feeling. The kind of love God has for us goes beyond our feeling and failure. It is unconditional.

Examples of unconditional love

You may wonder how a righteous God could tell Hosea to marry a woman like Gomer. Let us answer with the Word of God itself. In the Bible, the Lord made certain individuals examples for eternity of the nature of God's love. One of these examples is Abraham in Genesis 22:1-14. It was to Abraham that God gave a son of promise, Isaac. Then one day He told Abraham, "Take now your son, your only son Isaac, whom you love, and go to the land of Moriah, and offer him there as a burnt offering . . . ." (v. 2). So Abraham obediently took his son, and the wood for the offering, and went to the mountain. There he prepared the altar, put his Isaac on the altar, and had the knife ready to slay him. Right at that point, the Lord stopped him.

This account of Abraham is also something that cannot be comprehended by the human thought. Why would God tell Abraham to kill his son? The answer is that Abraham was a type, or picture, of God giving His own Son on the cross. In the same way, Hosea taking Gomer for a wife is to be a practical picture to us because it symbolizes the nature of God's unconditional love. It exemplifies that in the worst condition, we are the objects of His love. It proves to us that God loves sinners!

The depths of God's love and the depth of our corruption

Love and *sinners* are both general terms. But when you start detailing the love of God and the sinful condition of God's people who were loved by Him, these general terms take on new significance, new meaning. Let us now look at the condition of the ones who are the objects of God's unconditional love. To consider this point may seem somewhat negative because we must deal with several negative things related to the condition of God's people. But it is the very unveiling of the rottenness of our condition that causes us to understand the love of God in a deeper and greater way.

We may read the biographies and diaries of some of the Lord's servants in the past, such as David Brainard and also Jim Elliot, who was a modern-day martyr. These are the very ones we would esteem as loving the Lord so much. Yet when we look in their diaries at their daily accounts of interacting with the Lord, we see again and again their confessions of their rottenness, their vileness before the Lord, and their rebellious heart and disobedience. We can see that they realized how deep their corruption was. Yet at the same time, we see how the Lord was so intimate, so sweet, and so precious to them because of His mercy and because of His precious blood.

The closer something gets to the light, the more you see its real condition. For example, there may be dirt on my hand, but I do not see it. Yet when I put my hand up to the light, I see the dirt that has been there all the time. In the same way, God has completely known us — just as David says in Psalm 139 — God sees us and knows what has been there all the time. Often you may be surprised at what comes out of you. You did not expect yourself to react in a sinful, fleshly way. But God is not surprised at all. He knew what was in you all the time. So when we get into the light as He is in the light, we just see what He has already seen and known. Yet because of His great love and because of the blood, He has not withheld any fellowship or any love — He has not withheld anything of Himself. He just gives Himself because the blood is cleansing us from all sin (1 John 1:7).

On one hand, we see the depth of His love, and on the other hand, we see the depth of our corruption. We are confessing and admitting, yet we are also singing and enjoying that we, such vile sinners, can be washed in the precious blood and know the intimacies of the love of God in our heart. What a wonder! It is good for us to see the depths of corruption within our hearts so that we will enjoy in an even greater way the everlasting love of God, the incredible love of God, that is continuously with us. From such love Paul had to say he could not be separated (Rom. 8:35-39).

You have to consider God's love in this way — He has put us in Christ, the Beloved One. Ephesians 1:6 says, "He has made us accepted in the Beloved." Literally, this verse can be translated, "He has *graced* us in the Beloved." Usually you would consider the word "Beloved" to be a noun, referring to a person who is called "the Beloved One." However, in this verse "Beloved" is a participle, a verbal adjective.

The Beloved is also in the perfect tense, meaning that the *action* or *state of being* began at a point of time in the past and continues to be a present reality. The perfect tense can be thought of as a combination of three tenses — past, present, and future. Thus, "Beloved" could be translated "The One who is presently in the state of being loved." When the Lord Jesus is referred to in Ephesians 1:6 as *the Beloved,* it means He is the One who is continuously the object of the Father's love. "The Beloved" is not just describing Him as a person, but it is describing a state in which He exists this very minute — the state of being the object of the Father's love.

In this universe there is a current, a stream, of the love of the Father flowing, and this current is directed toward and "hitting" His Son. It is flowing from the Father to the Son, and again from the Son back to the Father in a continuous cycle. The Son is the Beloved, and He pours the love He receives from the Father back to the Father. It is an eternal "bosom life" that the Son has with the Father. He is "into the bosom of the Father" (John 1:18). He is the unique object of the Father's love. He is in that state this minute. Thus, there is a glorious love-life going on right now in the universe between the Father and the Son.

Not only so, but God has graced us in the beloved One. That means He has put us into Christ — into this One who is in this state of being loved. This current of love between the Father and the Son is like the movement of dotted lights that continuously cycle. We are all watching the love flowing between the Father and the Son, and between the Son and the Father. Then God put us in the Son! Now we are the objects of the Father's love. He has graced us in this beloved One. Because we are now in the Son, we too are the objects of the love of God.

The general condition of the objects of God's unconditional love

Let us look more closely at the objects that God's unconditional love is continuously directed toward. By seeing the condition of these objects, we can have more appreciation of the depths of the love of God. Surely we have already seen something of the nature of God's love in the example of Hosea marrying Gomer, "a wife of harlotry." Then we further appreciated God's love as it is depicted in Hosea continuing to love Gomer while she was committing adultery, while she was departing from him. In our experience there have been periods of time in which we too have departed from the Lord.

Departing from the Lord

The Christian life is a life of union and fellowship with the Lord. The normal life is to be one spirit with the Lord, to live Him, to live by Him, to hear His voice and obey, and to stay with Him, drawing from the riches of His grace. Thus, to become a Christian is simply to receive great "capital," so to speak, called "the exceeding riches of His grace" (Eph. 2:7) and then to spend those riches by contacting the Lord, staying with Him, and enjoying Him.

But what happens characteristically is that the devil attacks us. His goal is to cause us to depart from the Lord. Departing from the Lord is not initially a big outward departure. It is first of all an inward departing. Thus, the incipient stage is simply to depart from the enjoyment of the riches of Christ. It is not just a departure from mere patterns or habits we have built up, but it is a departure from drinking at the fountain and being in fellowship with the Lord (Jer. 2:13; John 4:14). We may inwardly get distracted just as Martha did in the Gospel of Luke. Our distraction may be with good things that preoccupy and usurp us. It does not have to be evil things that usurp us. Like Martha, we may be outwardly serving others, yet we have inwardly departed from our fellowship with the Lord. But Mary, in contrast to Martha, "chose the better part." She did not depart but sat at Jesus' feet. She just stayed with the Lord (Luke 10:38-42).

We have seen that the normal Christian life is a life of fellowship and enjoyment with the Lord. But we often get busy. We spend less and less time with the Lord, so there is less beholding of Him in the Word and in prayer. We neglect the means by which we receive the riches of His grace. Besides neglecting our own personal time with the Lord, we may also neglect corporate and fellowship gatherings. Whether it be a large meeting or a home meeting in twos or threes, we do not have much fellowship with others. We start departing, and then backsliding begins to take place in a very hidden, secret, progressive kind of way.

Thus, it is first an inward departing, which causes a breaking down of fellowship with the Lord. As a result there is not a continuous current of divine life coursing through our being — supplying our mind, supplying our emotions, supplying our will — energizing us to choose Him, to turn to Him. Isaiah 7:15 says, "Curds and honey He shall eat, that He may know to refuse the evil and choose the good." This prophecy is about Christ. "Curds and honey He shall eat" means He was nourished with the words from the Father. He was living by every word proceeding from the mouth of God (Matt. 4:4), that He would know to "refuse the evil and choose the good."

The Lord Jesus Himself in His humanity needed to live supplied from the Father. Then He intuitively knew what to reject and what to choose. This kind of knowing comes from living out of God as our source. It comes from being in fellowship with Him. Thus, when we lose that supply, what is left is our unsupplied self. We are left to ourselves, and the self has only one direction to go, and that is down — into self-centeredness and into the flesh. We are just left to whatever we are, to however our flesh expresses itself.

We can see from the Word of God and from our own personal experience that, when we inwardly depart from the Lord and His supply of grace, the result is an outward departure. For example, we may become loose about what we read and what we listen to. We may start speaking to others in a cruel way or even cheat others. When we were supplied we learned to refuse the evil, but without supply we just return to those same old ways. We outwardly depart.

Forsaking the fountain of living water

When Jeremiah spoke to God's people, telling them they were backsliders, he was speaking the same thing Hosea was speaking. Their years of ministry even overlapped to some degree. Jeremiah 2:13 says, "For My people have committed two evils: they have forsaken Me, the fountain of living waters, and hewn themselves cisterns." So we see that first they forsook the fountain, and then eventually they were in idolatry, in all kinds of outward departure.

This was the same situation in the book of Hosea. There God's people, symbolized by Gomer, had departed from Him. Then Hosea took his adulterous wife, Gomer, back again, expressing God's unchanging love to His people. If you are a departing one — whether you are in the stage of inwardly departing because you left the supply or in the stage of outwardly departing, doing things you never would have imagined when you were with the Lord — be assured that God has taken you as the object of His unchanging love. He still loves and pursues those who have departed.

If we are departing ones, we simply need to face the real situation and admit where we are. At the same time, we need to know that God's love is dependable to every departing one. If you have departed for one month, one year, or ten years, the love of God is toward you. All He will say to you is "Martha, Martha" (Luke 10:41). He will call you by your name and draw you with cords of love. He will speak to your heart, wooing you lovingly to Himself, getting you to look at yourself for a moment and to admit where you have been. He loves you, and then He loves you some more, until you find yourself saying, "What have I to do anymore with idols?" (Hosea 14:8). In other words, His love wins your heart. He is not coercing you. He is not barging in and forcibly saying, "Turn over your whole life to Me." If this were the situation, you would be gritting your teeth and trying to eke out that kind of willingness. No, He woos and wins your whole heart.

How awful it would be to have a marriage in which the husband is commanding his wife to love him: "You have to love me. The Bible says so." The poor wife is under that kind of relationship. That is not love. Love needs freedom because love is voluntary. Love is giving. "God is love" means that God is giving Himself. He is free to give Himself. In the same way, we love the Lord not by being under a law to love the Lord. We love the Lord because we are free to love the Lord. That is what love is. And this is the kind of relationship we need to cultivate with the Lord, even when we find ourselves departing from Him.

Backslidden

Now let us look further at the general condition of God's people who have departed from the Lord and are backsliding. The Bible uses the word *backsliding* to indicate a going back or a slipping back from the normal, proper state. The general condition of God's people who have departed from Him is revealed in Hosea's family. We have already seen that Hosea's wife was a harlot and that she continued in that sinful lifestyle after he married her. Then she bore Hosea a son, and God called his name Jezreel, which means "God will scatter." Next she bore a daughter named Lo-Ruhamah, meaning "no mercy," and a second son Lo-Ammi, meaning "not My people" (Hosea 1:4-9). These names show us that sometimes when God's love is revealed over His people, it is revealed in a way of seeming severity.

In some of the verses in Hosea, God's judgment is over His people, but always with the goal of turning their hearts back to Himself. Then before long, the love of God is again alluring them. This shows us that He is doing everything He can to win our hearts. He will try from one position to gain an entrance into our hearts and then again from another position. And if He still cannot, He will try in yet another way. His love is always coming to us in one way or another. In other words, whatever way God could break through our coldness, our hardness, and our indifference, it is always a form of His love coming to us. If it is a spanking, that too is His love to us. Who knows which way God's love will come to us!

Some of the names in Hosea are used by the Lord in a double sense. For example, Jezreel, "God will scatter," means the nation is scattered, seemingly no longer existing. Then later the Lord says that He will sow her again as Jezreel (Hosea 2:22-23). This time He is not using the name in a scattering sense but in the sense of sowing. The Hebrew word *Jezreel* means both "I will sow" and "I will scatter." The first mention of Jezreel meant a scattering, a dispersing; but the next mention meant a sowing in the earth with mercy. This again shows us what kind of God we are related to. This is His love. So here we can see Hosea's family revealing something of our condition, and affording God the opportunity to display more of the depths of His love toward the departing ones.

A decided point of departure

Now let us look more specifically at the various aspects of a backsliding condition. First, there is a decided point of departure. Hosea 2:5 says, "For their mother has played the harlot; she who conceived them has done shamefully. For she said, '*I will go* after my lovers, who give me my bread and my water, my wool and my linen, my oil and my drink.' " In Hebrew, the verb "I *will go*" indicates a definite, determined decision. It is saying, "I have made up my mind. I have inwardly resolved and determined that I am departing from the Lord and going after my lovers." This is rebellion, and this has been the condition not only of Gomer, but of God's people at various times in their history.

Maybe you have been with the Lord for a while, but things have not happened according to your expectation. So you are disappointed and perhaps disillusioned. Do not forget that all of this is a kind of test to you. Then at this point some "lover" comes along — a material thing, a relationship, your own goal or purpose. And you say within yourself, "I am not going to live for the Lord's interests anymore. I am going to go after my lovers who will give me my bread and my water — who will meet my needs. This life of trusting the Lord is too insecure.

I want to go where there is some security. I want someone who is going to love me and give me all the things that I need." So there is a departing from the Lord. We would analyze this condition and probably conclude that it is quite rebellious. But in this very condition, God loves you. You have not escaped the love of God. You said, "I will go after my lovers." And He said, "I will come after my beloved," because He has an investment in you. His Son, the Object of His love, is in your spirit, and you will never extract Him from you. He is there to stay. You may make your bed in hell, but you are there with Christ in you (Psa. 139:8), and God will seek you there because you are in His Son and therefore are the object of the Father's love. God has an eternal vested interest in your whole being — spirit, soul, and body —that you would be in the image of His Son. So God's love will find you wherever you go, even when you have determined to depart and go after other lovers.

This indeed is God's love. I can testify to this kind of love because I have had secret, hidden departures in my own life. But each time, what I have come back to again and again is the Lord's love. There is no way to escape His love. It is so wooing, so attractive, so irresistible. It is an irresistible love that brings us back to Himself. He still loves the one who at a certain point has decided to depart from Him.

In Revelation 2:4-5 the Lord speaks to the church at Ephesus: 4 "Nevertheless I have this against you, that you have left your first love. 5 Remember therefore from where you have fallen; repent and do the first works." In other words, there was a point of departure in which these believers made a decision to go after something else. So the Lord comes and tells them to repent, to come back. This is all the Lord's love to us.

Living two lives

As we continue in Hosea we see that those who departed from the Lord had a false, superficial lifestyle. This was their condition. In Hosea 2:11 the Lord says, "I will also cause all her mirth to cease, her feast days, her New Moons, her Sabbaths — all her appointed feasts." Here the word "mirth" refers to superficial silliness. Then the Lord continues in verses 12-13, [12] And I will destroy her vines and her fig trees, of which she has said, 'These are my rewards that my lovers have given me.' So I will make them a forest, and the beasts of the field shall eat them. [13] I will punish her for the days of the Baals to which she burned incense. She decked herself with her earrings and jewelry, and went after her lovers. Then she forgot Me, says the Lord." This describes a lifestyle that has a double standard. In one breath, she was keeping all the appointed feasts and celebrating the New Moons and Sabbaths. Apparently, she was quite spiritual. But then, in the next breath, she had departed from the Lord and was living in an idolatrous and ungodly way.

In her life there was a double standard, not a single standard. In like manner, we may profess to be a Christian, a church-attending believer. But we have one standard for being around people in that setting, and another standard in our personal life. We are living a dual lifestyle. Sometimes we may hear that not all the servants of the Lord on this earth live with a single standard. But it is so touching to know that through the years some have kept themselves from duality. They continue to have a single standard, and when you read about their life you discover that what they are in public — "on the platform" so to speak — is what they are in their home. In other words, they are not living two lives.

But suppose you are a person with a kind of false lifestyle, living two lives. One life is coming to the Christian meetings and doing all the outward things; but separate from that is your other life, in which you are going after other "lovers." Humanly speaking, we all know that this is despicable. But if that is where you are right now, God is stooping to meet you there and to love you back to Himself. Yes, His love comes to this condition.

The love of God is incredible! To us it seems too good to be true. You thought you were "beyond the point of no return" because you have been practicing a double standard for many years. You would never outwardly give up the Lord, but inwardly you have gone after other lovers. However, the Lord will take you out of Egypt (the world) and bring you into the wilderness for a time (Hosea 2:14). He will put you in a situation where He can allure you and start talking to your heart. He will begin to single your heart to love just Him and to live Him. He does all this by securing your cooperation. This is how He works — "with the grain," so to speak, and not against it. The guarantee of the New Covenant is this: [26] "I [the Lord] will give you a new heart and put a new spirit within you; I will take the heart of stone out of your flesh and give you a heart of flesh. [27] I will put My Spirit within you and cause you to walk in My statutes" (Ezek. 36:26-27). He will do it by His Spirit. This is His way of coming to you and loving you in your kind of condition.

Loving substitutes

Hosea 3:1 is a key verse for understanding the nature of the book of Hosea. In this verse Hosea says, "Then the LORD said to me, Go again, love a woman who is loved by a lover [her husband, Hosea] and is committing adultery, just like the love of the LORD for the children of Israel, who look to other gods and love the raisin cakes of the pagans." Here is a condition that could be described as loving things that are substitutes for God: loving "the raisin cakes *of the pagans.*" Brothers and sisters, do you realize that we are living in a pagan society? Paganism and godlessness is all around us and is seeking to infiltrate our lives every single day through the radio, through the television, through the newspapers, through professors, through the concepts, views, values, and lifestyles of other people. In other words, through all these means the devil is trying to cause us to conform to the world's values, the world's styles, and the world's ways.

Here in Hosea, God's people are loving the raisin cakes of the pagans — the things that belong to the pagans. Perhaps the source of our values is not so much the Word of God but television shows or some other form of entertainment. Do you realize that you are constantly forming your values based upon what you take in — what you watch, what you read and hear? For example, you may be relating to your husband or wife according to what you have learned from the pagans and not according to the Word of God.

So here we are — with our views, our thoughts, and our values. Where did we learn these things? From God? Were we taught by the Spirit? Does the Lord allow what we do, or does our generation allow it? This touches all of us. But even if our whole value system is filled with pagan ideas and views, and not what God values, His love still comes to us in this condition. When we have substituted other things for the Lord, and those things have become the objects of our love, even then the Lord comes to draw us to Himself.

Periods of utter void

As the Lord is drawing us away from substitutes and back to Himself, we may experience periods of utter void. This is the situation in Hosea 3:3-4. In verse 3 Hosea says to his wife, Gomer, "You shall stay with me many days; you shall not play the harlot, nor shall you have a man; thus I will also be toward you." Then the Lord interprets what this means for His people: "For the children of Israel shall abide many days without king or prince, without sacrifice or sacred pillar, without ephod or teraphim." Verse 3 refers to a time when the wife was taken away from her lovers and when she also did not have the intimacy of her husband. The Lord was taking her through a period in which she had no more lovers, no more things to satisfy the sensual pleasures of the flesh. She could not fulfill her lust anymore; she could not have that kind of lifestyle anymore. And neither could she have a full intimate love relationship with her husband. She was just existing there, utterly void.

While you are in this condition of utter void, the Lord is right there loving you. He says, "I will also be toward you." He will love you, but He is not going to manifest so much of His love to your feelings right now. He is "behind the curtains," so to speak, but still toward you, still loving you. He is unseen but loving you. Here you are in a period of backlash in which you cannot fulfill your lust over here, and you do not have full satisfaction over there. So you are experiencing frustration and utter void. This often happens when you have plunged into the flesh, plunged into sin — you get the backlash of it. You just feel empty, disgusted, and utterly void. You have no feeling, no real enjoyment, but just a barrage of condemning thoughts. While you are in that condition, the Lord is right there saying, "I am toward you. I am loving you in this. My love has not diminished toward you, but I have not yet manifested it to you."

During this kind of period, the Lord operates in our being just as He did in the prodigal son in Luke 15:11-24. This young man had left home and plunged himself into riotous living. He spent all his inheritance fulfilling the lusts of his flesh. Then, being "in want" he took a job feeding swine. So he went from extravagant, wasteful living to a life of poverty and hunger. All the glamour had dissipated. Sin always has this effect — it dissipates. Hebrews 11:25 speaks of enjoying "the pleasures of sin for a season" (KJV). Some versions translate this phrase, "the *passing* pleasures of sin." The pleasure is only for a season.

Finally, in his dissipated condition, the prodigal son "came to himself." While he was in a period of utter void and emptiness, he realized that it was really better at home with his father. So he said to himself, "I will arise and go to my father." He set out for home with a rehearsed confession and proposal to his father. He was feeling his unworthiness as a son and the utter void of having nothing to show for his time away in sin. In this condemned state, feeling like the worst kind of son, he came to his father.

But the father saw him while he was "still a great way off." Now, notice the father's style of loving. He did not wait until his son arrived at the doorstep. But upon seeing him, he "had compassion, and ran and fell on his neck and kissed him." Then he clothed him with the best robe, put a ring on his hand and sandals on his feet, and prepared the fatted calf to celebrate his homecoming. That is the style of God's love.

Consider God's love in our own experience. When you and I can barely say, "I love You, Lord" — when we do not have that much feeling — but we gather with other believers or have some fellowship with a brother or sister — God in His love runs to meet us, lavishing His love upon us. This is His love to us in our periods of utter void. He is there as He promised: "I will be toward you." He is still loving, still toward us in this period.

Breaking all restraint

Now let us consider another aspect of a backsliding condition — breaking all restraint. Hosea 4:2 describes this condition: "By swearing and lying, killing and stealing and committing adultery, they break all restraint, with bloodshed after bloodshed." In this condition there are no restraints. One sin is added to another sin. All of this makes us realize what a wonderful thing it is that we human beings have a conscience. Even ungodly people, unbelieving people, have a conscience; and many unbelievers do live by their conscience the best they know how. Our conscience is precious because it is a restraining influence on man's flesh, restraining it from breaking out in violence and immorality. Of course, the law enforcement agencies in our country also act as a restraining influence upon man's sinful, rebellious flesh.

Here in Hosea 4:2 God's people broke all restraint. They were lying, killing, and committing adultery. Because there was no restraint, there was bloodshed upon bloodshed. This was their condition. They had silenced their conscience, not wanting to listen to it anymore.

In the New Testament, the apostle Paul uses several different words to describe the breaking of all restraint: *uncleanness, fornication,* and *unbridled greedy lust* (Gal. 5:19; Eph. 4:19; 5:3; Col. 3:5). Then he also uses the word *sensuality,* which best describes the breaking of all moral restraints. It denotes doing things openly, even condoning what God hates. Together these words describe what happened with God's people in the book of Hosea. They broke all restraints. This also describes what has happened morally to this country.

Perhaps you feel this way about yourself — that you have added one sin upon another. You have broken restraint, you have silenced your conscience. In these periods the devil does a lot of talking in your mind, and in his talking he draws the conclusion that once and for all you are reprobate. He tells you that you are past any hope because you have broken the restraint. But again, God's love comes into this kind of situation. He says of His people, "I will allure her, I will heal her backsliding. I will love her freely." What can He do with Ephraim? Can He give her up? Can He hand her over? No, He cannot do that. He can only love her.

This is the unconditional love of God toward the objects of His love. He loves us in a personal way. He said, "Jacob have I loved." So He loves you by name. He loves me by name. Regardless of being a failure and a mass of corruption — regardless of all these things — we are the objects of His love.

Rejecting light

Finally, let us look at the matter of rejecting light, another aspect of a backsliding condition. Hosea 4:6 says, "My people are destroyed for lack of knowledge. Because you have rejected knowledge..." God's people rejected knowledge, they rejected the Word, they rejected light. Many times in the church life we have talked about God's light coming and about walking in the light while we have the light. Yet much of the time we have not walked in the light while we had it. Instead, we rejected the light. Yes, God did speak to us; but we did not *listen*. Now those lingering failures in our experience become the raw material the devil uses to categorize and accuse us. He will use lingering defeats, injecting accusing thoughts of what we passed through, to taunt us and eventually categorize us.

The Greek word for "accuser" is *kategoros* (κατήγορος), from which we get the word *category*. This indicates that the nature of the devil's work is to put us into a category. He will say to you, "You are just this kind of person. You will never be any different. This is the way you have always been and this is the way you will continue to be." Then you begin looking at yourself according to how he is categorizing you. Eventually you say, "This is the way I am. I might as well give up." Many suicides today are simply due to the devil succeeding in convincing people's minds that there is no hope for them because they have rejected God at some point. But in the book of Hosea, God's love comes to His people who have rejected knowledge, who have rejected light. God spoke through the Old Testament prophets, again and again revealing His love. He came to these people to woo, to love, and to do whatever He could to secure the mutual love He desired. And one day He will obtain His heart's desire — that mutual, reciprocal love from His people.

Nothing separating us from the love of God

In Hosea 2:23 the Lord says, "Then I will sow her for Myself in the earth [this is the positive meaning of the name Jezreel], and I will have mercy on her who had not obtained mercy; then I will say to those who were not My people, 'You are My people!' And they shall say, 'You are my God!'" This is what the love of God does to us fallen, corrupt, rebellious, light-rejecting people. He comes to us, secures our heart, and then says, "You are My people!"

In 1 Corinthians 6:11 Paul says to the believers, "And such were some of you." Some of us were drunkards, homosexuals, fornicators, covetous, extortioners. Yet Paul continues, "But you were washed, but you were sanctified, but you were justified in the name of the Lord Jesus and by the Spirit of our God." So God has taken each of us who were a "mass of corruption" and made us the objects of His love. He has wooed us and won us, and now we say, "You are my God." Hallelujah! This is the reality of the church — a group of people enjoying this love.

May the Holy Spirit take these words and expand our revelation of the nature of God's love toward us so that we could never be the same. Under this revelation, we can say with Paul, "*in* all these things we are more than conquerors through Him who loved us" — *in* tribulation, *in* distress, *in* persecution, *in* famine, *in* nakedness, *in* peril, *in* sword (Rom. 8:37, 35). This unconditional love of God persuades us that nothing — no, nothing! — can separate us from God coming to us, drawing us, wooing us, and winning these hearts of ours from whatever has held them captive. We are secure in this love, so we can go on enjoying this love. Then God's purpose is accomplished — He obtains a group of people who overcome the accuser of the brethren by the blood of the Lamb (Rev. 12:10-11). That blood is a great testimony in the whole heavenly realm, that there was a day in this universe when God demonstrated His love. He proved His love by shedding His own blood for sinners. While we were sinners, Christ died for us.

One day we are all going to be transferred to another realm to have another festal gathering. We are meeting here on earth, and we will be meeting again in resurrection. We are going to meet with all the saints, and for eternity we are all going to shout, "It's the blood! It's the blood!" This is the love of God coming through the blood of Jesus, washing and cleansing us sinners to be right with Him and to enjoy Him. And He will say, "You are My people!" And we will say, "You are our God!"

3

The Extent of God's Unconditional Love

God opens up His heart to us in the book of Hosea to show us the extent of His unconditional love. Probably no other book in the Bible so details the love of God as this book. Yet we need the Spirit's convincing work to show us how the love of God is unveiled here. When we first read Hosea's fourteen chapters, we may wonder what we could glean of God's love from this book. But as we open up to the Lord and spend time in this word, the Holy Spirit will indeed reveal to us that this is a book of God's unconditional love.

God's love determines our relationships

As believers we may talk about God's love and know about God's love, yet in our experience over the years we may have related to the Lord based upon something other than God's love. So we must see that our whole relationship with the Lord is based upon His unconditional love toward us, and that this love is continuous, eternal, and cannot be frustrated by anything. It is this love that determines how we feel about the Lord, how we feel about ourself, and how we feel about one another. God's love determines all of this.

It is God's love that determines our relationships with one another. His love is the highest sphere in which we could be related. It is God's desire that His people on the earth express relationships in the love of God. The Lord said it in this way in John 13:35: "By this all will know that you are My disciples, if you have love for one another." By this the world will know. This love is what identifies us as His disciples. This is what testifies that we belong to Him — there is a quality of love that exists between one another that cannot be found in any other place. This is God's unconditional love that flows like a river, and that should flow among His people. The more we touch the revelation of this love, the more the light will shine on our relationships as members of one another in the Body of Christ. First Corinthians 8:1 clearly speaks of building up one another *in love*. This reveals that the element of our building is love.

The revelation of this love begins with the Lord joining Himself to His chosen people in spite of their utter corruption, fallen humanity, and sinful condition. This is all graphically depicted in the first chapter of the book of Hosea. Then in the following chapters we see that not only *initially* does God love us as sinful persons, but He *continues* to love us in our condition, whatever it may be. We can see that God's unconditional love is directed toward us in our condition of being totally sinful, corrupt, and failing. Out of God's heart, out of His selection, He has chosen to beam His love into this kind of person. This revelation stops our reasoning mind in its tracks, and opens us up in spirit to have an unveiling of what God's love is all about. His love is not conditional. It is not based upon our condition but upon His free giving: "I will love them freely."

God's love and the details of our condition

By seeing all the details of the horrible condition of the ones God is loving, we will not be mistaken about God's love directed toward us. To speak about God's love in a general way may not touch our heart. But the book of Hosea speaks of God's love coming to *specific* rebellious conditions that His people were found in. It was in those conditions, described in detail, that He drew them with bands of love and allured them. This helps us realize that God's love is directed toward us in our specific condition.

Influenced by corrupt examples

Let us look at more details of our condition that God, in His love, comes to. Hosea 4:6-9 says, [6] "My people are destroyed for lack of knowledge. Because you have rejected knowledge, I also will reject you from being priest for Me; because you have forgotten the law of your God, I also will forget your children. [7] The more they increased, the more they sinned against Me; I will change their glory into shame. [8] They eat up the sin of My people; they set their heart on their iniquity. [9] And it shall be: like people, like priest."

These verses show us that we can have an influence upon one another. Here the influence was corrupt and sinful. God's people were being influenced by corrupt examples, as described in the words "like people, like priest." The whole level of their walk with the Lord was lowered. Everyone's life was lowered because they took one another as the standard and example to follow. Some saw others giving themselves over to other loves, and instead of following the Lord, they followed the others' example. This is how everyone was pulled down. "Like people, like priest" tells us that the people followed the degraded example of the priest, and the priest followed the degraded condition of the people. Thus they followed one another in their sinfulness and in their rebellion.

This may happen in our own experience. Perhaps there are certain people in our life that we look up to. In the world today they are called role models. When the person that we look up to backslides, if our own heart is not steadfast on the Lord, we ourselves will veer from Him. We may lose heart and even give up the Christian life. In Hosea 4 this was the kind of interaction going on between the people and the priest. They were influenced by each other's corrupt example. This was the condition of Israel. Yet it is to these kinds of people the Lord comes in His love and says, "I will heal their backsliding, I will love them freely" (Hosea 14:4).

Ceasing to obey the Lord

Hosea 4:10 says, "They shall commit harlotry, but not increase; because they have ceased obeying the Lord." This means they stopped obeying the Lord, they stopped obeying His life. This was their condition. You may have passed through this same kind of experience many times. Something happens in your life to dishearten you, to disillusion you. You were following the Lord, you were loving Him and pursuing

Him. But something interrupted your fellowship with the Lord and removed you from the love of God. Then you were precipitated into a loose, disobedient life, not following the impulses of the divine life within you.

Normally, God's life is flowing in us all day long. He is living and flowing in us as we enjoy Him, follow Him, and just obey Him. But if something has happened to cause you to stop following the Lord and to cease obeying Him, God still loves you. And He wants to draw and woo and win you back to Himself. Yours is the kind of condition that God's love is directed toward. This further reveals to us the *extent* of God's unconditional love toward His people.

Possessed with a spirit of harlotry

In Hosea 4:11 and 12 we see that God's people were possessed with a spirit of harlotry: [11] "Harlotry, wine, and new wine enslave the heart. . . . [12] For the spirit of harlotry has caused them to stray, and they have played the harlot against their God." God's love is also toward those who are possessed with a spirit of harlotry. Let us look at our own experience. Many times there is one disobedience that precipitates us into a spirit of disobedience. Perhaps you did not follow the Lord, and then a spirit of straying seemed to possess you and take you away from the Lord. There you were, possessed with a disobedient spirit, living in a kind of spiritual adultery. After passing through periods like this, you are left with a barrage of accusation. You may feel, "God, this is it. There is no hope." The one disobedience was bad enough, but to be possessed with a spirit that propelled you into a life of disobedience was too much to bear. But the Lord has joined Himself to the ones who are possessed with a spirit of harlotry in order to express His unconditional love, to woo and win them back.

Hosea 2:5-7 shows us the Lord's marvelous way of expressing His love to those who have a spirit of harlotry. Verse 5 describes this spirit of harlotry: "For she said, I will go after my lovers." This describes a spirit of harlotry. "I will go after my lovers, who give me my bread and my water, my wool and my linen, my oil and my drink." This means she is living in this way. To the one in this condition, the Lord says in verses 6-7, [6] "Therefore, behold, I will hedge up your way with thorns, and wall her in, so that she cannot find her paths. [7] She will chase her lovers, but not overtake them; yes, she will seek them, but not find them. Then she will say, I will go and return to my first husband, for then it was better for me than now." This is God's hedging-up love and His walling-in love.

God's love comes even to those who have a spirit of harlotry, who are precipitated into a life of disobedience in which they cannot stop. For example, you may have eyes that "cannot cease from sin" (2 Pet. 2:14). You would like to stop your eyes, but they will not stop. So God's love comes in the form of hedging up your way with thorns. He says, "Therefore, behold, I will hedge up your way with thorns." This means that as you are pursuing your lovers, as you are on the pathway of indulging yourself, there are some "thorns" pricking you on the way.

There are some unpleasant things that happen on the road to sin. The Lord hedges up our way with thorns. It is not smooth. It is not what we thought it was going to be. And the more we have the spirit of harlotry — the more we are pursuing that course — the more the love of God comes in and everything seems to go wrong. Or as verse 6 says, the Lord will "wall her in, so that she cannot find her paths." So God's love walls us in. Then it seems we are walking about in a maze.

You may have some dear ones, some family members or friends, who have made a determination to follow their lovers and go another way, leaving the Lord. The best way to pray for them is to ask the Lord to hedge up their way with thorns and wall them in so that they will not find their pathway. Then they will chase their lovers, but not overtake them. Finally, God's love so frustrates their path of harlotry that they end up with a consciousness that says, "I will go and return to my first husband, for then it was better for me than now" (2:7). This is God's love. God's love is in the thorns and in the walls. So we see how much the Lord cares for us. We can never escape this unconditional kind of love, even when we are possessed with a spirit of harlotry. This shows us more of the extent of God's unconditional love.

Being stubborn and rebellious

Now let us look at another condition, the condition of being stubborn and rebellious. In Hosea 5:4-5 the description of God's people leaves you with the impression that they refused to turn to God. They were filled with pride. Then verse 6 says, "With their flocks and herds they shall go to seek the LORD, but they will not find Him; He has withdrawn Himself from them." This indicates they were desperately trying to find God, but He had withdrawn Himself. Then they made a shallow commitment, as the Lord describes in Hosea 6:4: "O Ephraim, what shall I do to you? O Judah, what shall I do to you? For your faithfulness is like a morning cloud, and like the early dew it goes away." Sometimes you may have felt this way — just shallow, not very faithful to the Lord. It is just as He describes, "like a morning cloud." This was the condition of the children of Israel. But in this whole situation, even with its words of judgment, what is pervading is the Lord's faithful, eternal, and everlasting love.

Deliberate and planned sin

In Hosea 6:7-10 God's people are described as deliberately defiling His promised land. And in chapter 7, verses 1-3, they were blinded by the effect of sin. Furthermore, verses 4-7 tell us that they were actually planning and waiting to sin. Their sin had gone to this point. No doubt, we know that sin has operated in our being just like that. It plans and it plots and it waits. And when those kinds of things surface in our being, we surely have the feeling that we are not loved by the Lord. In this condition, unless God reveals His love to us, we are just left to ourselves. But again, it is to this kind of condition that God comes and shows His love.

Refusing to call upon the Lord

In Hosea 7:7 the Lord says, "There is none among them who calls upon Me." They refused to call on Him. Sometimes in our own experience, we have not called on the Lord, even though He has made Himself so available to us through His name. It is normal to enjoy calling on the Lord. When we call, He is rich to us (Rom. 10:12).

Insensitive to God's discipline

In Hosea 7:8-16 God's people were insensitive to His discipline. God came to them and tried to speak to them, but they ignored His hand and His discipline. They were presumptuous. They lost all spiritual principles. They broke out in their flesh without restraint, leaving every kind of spiritual principle they had lived by. And they gave themselves over to idolatry. Nothing was governing them. They just left it all.

Wandering from God's house

Hosea 9:1-6 and 11-17 describes God's people as living a life of wandering away from God's house. They lost all hope because of the corruption of the prophets, and they themselves were changed into shameful affections (Hosea 9:10). They became an embodiment and personification of the very things they were worshiping — their idols, their fornication, and their harlotry. They were changed into these shameful affections. This was their condition.

The backlash of guilt

Then Hosea 10:8 says, "They shall say to the mountains, 'Cover us!' And to the hills, 'Fall on us!' " After so much sin and so much rebellion, they wanted to hide, and they wanted to end their life. They wanted to give up. This kind of reaction is the backlash, the end result, of so much guilt. They were trusting not in the Lord but in false supports (10:13). They despitefully rejected God's call (11:2). His speaking came to them through the prophets and they rejected it. They refused to repent (11:5). They were bent on backsliding (11:7; 14:4), filled with lies and deceit (11:12; 12:1), and living with a false security (12:8). They provoked God (12:14). There was constant sinning (13:2, 12). They went through sorrows because of vacillating with the Lord (13:13). The kickback of their iniquity is that they kept stumbling and being offended over and over again (14:1). This is the kickback that we get from living lawlessly and apart from God. We are offended and we repeatedly stumble as a result of living a lawless life. This was the condition of the ones that God's love was directed toward.

It is helpful to describe the content of these verses because it identifies so many specific areas and conditions that God's love comes to. Otherwise, we might say, "Well, God can love this person, and God can love that person, but God cannot love me because I have gone beyond the limits, beyond the reach, of His love." But look at Israel. She became so corrupt, so rebellious. Her condition was embodied in Gomer — the totality of failure, the completion and epitome of corruption.

It is to this woman that the Lord sends Hosea, saying, "Go, take yourself a wife of harlotry" (1:2), and "Go again, love a woman who is loved by a lover [her husband, Hosea] and is committing adultery, just like the love of the LORD for the children of Israel, who look to other gods and love the raisin cakes of the pagans" (3:1). May this verse — Hosea 3:1 — be written on our heart, because it is a clear revelation of God's unconditional love directed toward the most hopeless condition.

Quieted in God's love

Zephaniah 3:17 also reveals the effect that God's unconditional love has on us: "The LORD your God in your midst, the Mighty One, will save; He will rejoice over you with gladness, *He will quiet you in His love,* He will rejoice over you with singing." The effect of His love is to quiet us. So in any kind of condition — whatever our condition may be — we just need to be in His presence with His love, and He will calm our every fear, our every care.

Come into His presence with all the noise of your mind, your condemned feelings, your failures — with the noise of it all — just come, and He will quiet you in His love. This means we can simply enjoy being in His presence and opening ourselves to Him, knowing that His precious blood has been shed for us and is cleansing us from all sin. Because we know that we can never go beyond the reach of the love of God, we will always be secure in that love, and our whole relationship with the Lord will be characterized by His love. Regardless of what kind of condition we find ourselves in, our relationship will be characterized by security in His love.

This consciousness of the love of God will begin to pervade our heart more and more so that our relationship with the Lord is not characterized by fear. With fear there is torment, there is agony; but "perfect love casts out fear" (1 John 4:18). Then our whole relationship with the Lord is characterized by love, security, and the confidence that our one need is simply to make contact with Him by calling upon His name (Zeph. 3:19), and to enjoy that love that has been poured out in our hearts (Rom. 5:5). We will not take any fearful thoughts from the enemy or any kind of negative, self-condemning thoughts. We will be quieted and secure in His love.

God's intrinsic love for us

In John 15:9 the Lord says, "As the Father loved Me, I also have loved you; abide in My love." Just stay in His love. Do not leave it. Remain there. We are not just *hoping* that God loves us. He intrinsically feels this way toward us. His intrinsic feeling of love is eternally flowing because of the finality of the cross. Because of the finality of what happened on our behalf at Calvary with the shedding of the Lord's blood, the Father has once and for all received us fallen, sinful people. God so intrinsically loved the world that He gave His only begotten Son (John 3:16). And He demonstrated that love: "While we were yet sinners, Christ died for us" (Rom. 5:8).

Because of Christ, God betrothed us to Himself "in righteousness and justice" (Hosea 2:19). He entered into a love relationship in righteousness, making Christ our imputed, legal righteousness and taking us out of our own standing. Now we are clothed with Christ Himself as our righteousness. So our love relationship with the Lord is based upon Him being our righteousness. God has betrothed us in justice. He judged our sins once and for all. On the cross, all our sins — past, present, and future — were laid on Christ. The sin question has been answered conclusively at Calvary. This is all tied in to God's unconditional love. This is how I am related to Him. My relationship is characterized by that love based upon blood — based upon God's righteousness and justice.

God betrothed us not only in righteousness and in justice, but also "in lovingkindness and mercy" (Hosea 2:19). Now God's intrinsic feeling toward us can only be love, because of Jesus, because of blood. Our whole relationship with Him is characterized by this — "God loves me."

God's demonstrated love

God's unconditional love in the book of Hosea is unveiled to us as we spend time in all the verses describing the negative conditions of God's people, as well as all the verses describing God's love. Now let us dwell on more aspects of the revelation of His love. As we previously pointed out, this love is demonstrated love. God's love was demonstrated, in type, with Hosea taking Gomer as his wife. In the New Testament, God's love was demonstrated to us on the cross. Thus, His love has been proved in an absolute way. This is the kind of love we have — it is demonstrated love.

God's shocking love

The love of God is also shocking love. Hosea 1:10 says, "Yet the number of the children of Israel shall be as the sand of the sea, which cannot be measured or numbered. And it shall come to pass in the place where it was said to them, 'You are not My people,' there it shall be said to them, 'You are the sons of the living God.'"

The book of Hosea is full of paradoxes. On one hand, God says, "You are not My people." And then He immediately says, "In the place where it was said to them, 'You are not My people,' there it shall be said to them, 'You are the sons of the living God.'" Praise the Lord! We are not only God's people, we are His sons! This is a kind of shocking love! We had just concluded that there was no way for us to be His people. The decision had been made. We thought we were left without God. But in the place where we felt we were left without God, there it shall be said, "You are the sons of the living God."

We are His sons because He imparted His life into us. The unique design of God's love is not only to forgive us and reconcile us to Himself but also to make us sons, and that means to fill us with life. Where it says that we were not His people, it does not say that we became His people. It actually says something higher and greater: "You are the sons of the living God." This means we have received divine life.

Love that makes us alive in Christ

Ephesians 2:1-3 are verses describing Gomer. When you

read them you see failure, a mass of corruption, spoiled humanity — living in the lusts of the flesh, fulfilling the desires of the flesh, and being by nature the children of wrath, even as the rest of mankind. But what immediately follows this description are verses 4 and 5: [4] "But God, who is rich in mercy, because of His great love with which He loved us, [5] even when we were dead in trespasses, made us alive together with Christ (by grace you have been saved)." Do you see what the real salvation is here? The real salvation is to be made alive together with Christ, that is, to receive life and be joined to life. The real salvation is to be one spirit with the Lord, who is a life-giving Spirit in our spirit (1 Cor. 6:17; 15:45).

So to this mass of corruption, the love of God comes with mercy. And what the love and mercy does is make us alive together with Christ, bringing us out of the realm of death into the realm of life. First, God loves us; and then He makes us alive together with Christ. Following this, we are saved by grace. We may think of salvation as merely escaping hell and going to heaven. Although this is a fact — we have eternal life — the real nature of this salvation is that we are made alive together with Christ. We are sons of the living God. The Lord's desire today is that through His love and our enjoyment of His love, He would make us people enjoying His life, living by His life, and expressing His life as sons.

What the church is

This is what the church is — a group of sons filled with

God's life, and living by that life day by day. First of all, we enjoy the life. We enjoy the riches, the surplus, and the capital of the life that we have in the Godhead. All the riches of God — the Father in the Son flowing as the Spirit — are now available for us to enjoy. And then, out of this enjoyment, we are brought into the realm of living by that life.

As we live by His life, we are continually passing through death and coming up in resurrection. For example, in your relationship with your husband, you experience many cycles of death and resurrection. In your relationship to your anxieties, you experience death and resurrection. In your relationship to your feelings of bitterness and lingering sorrow, you experience more death and resurrection. By saying "O Lord Jesus" from your spirit, you are, by the Spirit, putting to death the practices of your body (Rom. 8:13). All those outbreaks of your autonomous, independent self-life are being put to death. Whatever form the self may take, you say, "O Jesus, You are my life. Hallelujah, Lord. Thank You for death and resurrection."

Sometimes there is immediate resurrection, other times delayed resurrection. You may be there in death for a period of time. You have no sensation, no feeling, no inspiration, but you are still saying, "Amen, Lord. I am one with You, just one with You." And then you enjoy resurrection in the next days. This is how the church comes forth — by all of us enjoying God's life in this way in all the details of our daily living.

The purpose of God's love is to bring us into a life of sonship, to make us "sons of the living God" (Hosea 1:10). This is shocking love — that we "children of wrath" could be reached by God's rich mercy and made alive together with Christ. Here is this rebellious, sinful person who has been captured by the love of God, joined together with Christ, and is now living by His life and being saved in His life.

In these books of Hosea and Ephesians, God's economy of conforming us to the image of God's Son is clearly unveiled. This economy shows us that God's love has one thing in mind — to bring us into the enjoyment of His life. So you come to a meeting of the church and there is something flowing. It is something enjoyable, something you can drink of in the singing, something you can participate in. Where does that "something" come from? It is coming from the life supply of the Spirit in the spirits of the saints. In any church, in any assembly of believers, for that life supply to be present in the atmosphere of the meetings, it only requires a handful of saints who will live by God's life in their daily living — who will live in death and resurrection all day long, experiencing Christ. This brings in a solid supply for the whole church that we can all drink of and benefit from.

You cannot just come together in a church gathering and "work up" this life supply. This genuine flow of God's life in the meetings comes from you and I experiencing Christ during the week — at our desk at work, in our schedule at school, in our relationships at home — with all our problems and anxieties. In our daily living we are learning to meet everything with Christ, with His life, by applying our spirit. We are living by Another life. Then when we come together, there is a spontaneous life supply.

Love and life

God's love leads us to this life, and this life always leads us to the love. It is a constant reciprocal relationship — love and life, life and love. We are simply enjoying this cycle in a continuous way. You may not have lived by His life very much, but, hallelujah, you can be brought to His love, quieted in His love, and wooed and won until you find yourself saying, "What have I to do anymore with idols?" This is how the book of Hosea ends. After being joined to idols, left to himself, without hope, stubborn and rebellious — after all of this — at the end of the book, Ephraim now says, "What have I to do anymore with idols?" How did Ephraim get from one point to the other? It was by enjoying God's love, and then, by that love, being infused with God's life. God's life spontaneously does not care for idols. The not caring for idols is in the life. It is in the life supply. How marvelous this love is.

Gathering love

The issue of this life supply, of this enjoyment of life, is described in Hosea 1:11: "Then the children of Judah and the children of Israel shall be gathered together, and appoint for themselves one head; and they shall come up out of the land, for great will be the day of Jezreel!" Then in the next verse the Lord says, "Say to your brethren, My people, and to your sisters, Mercy is shown" (Hosea 2:1). The greatest manifestation of mercy to us is this — He gathers us together and becomes our unique living Head. Of course, we know that this word applies to the future of the nation of Israel. But the apostles, such as Peter and Paul, also applied these kinds of verses, especially Hosea 1:10, directly to the church, the Body of Christ.

During the time Hosea was written, the children of Judah and the children of Israel were divided. Israel was in the north with ten tribes, and Judah was in the south with two tribes. The God-ordained worship center was in Jerusalem in the south, but the northern tribes set up two independent centers, Bethel and Dan, in the north. To this divided condition, God said, "You are not My people." The whole situation was negative. But the Lord prophesies, "In the place where it was said to them, 'You are not My people,' there it shall be said to them, 'You are the sons of the living God'" (Hosea 1:10).

They are sons by God Himself becoming their life. Then they will be gathered together and appoint for themselves one head (Hosea 1:11). This means that out of God's life flows a church life, a Body life, a corporate life — a life in which we are gathered together enjoying the one Head dispensing all His riches to every member. The riches of His dispensing include both life supply and function — many and various kinds of function. This is all the Lord's mercy to us! What a mercy that He would take us divided, separated peoples and gather us together to one living Head, the Lord Jesus Christ.

Thus, flowing out of God's love is God's life and God's building. God's economy in the New Testament issues out of a people enjoying the unconditional love of God. By enjoying this love, we are filled with life and we gather and have fellowship. It is wonderful that we can have fellowship with all believers that have the enjoyment of this life. And the more we enjoy this life, the more there will be the same response in us that was found in Ephraim: "What have I to do anymore with idols?" We also as believers will say, "What have I to do with my worldly background and my division — what have I to do with these things?" Because of love and life, we spontaneously have the inward sense, "What have I to do with that?"

Vertical and horizontal love

Between us as believers we have the enjoyment of God's life with His unconditional love. We have received His life, and our relationship with Him is based on His love. The more we enjoy His life and love, the more secure we are in it. We know how His love works toward us. We are wretched, corrupt, sinful failures, yet God loves us because of Jesus. Individually, you and I know our relationship with God in this way, and together we can know this same love with each other. We can receive one another regardless of our condition or the things we are passing through. The love of God is flowing between us as believers horizontally, as well as between God and us vertically. There is horizontal love — forgiving love, forbearing love, merciful love, love that allows the Spirit to work in one another, love that receives one another unconditionally while we are all in the process of being transformed.

Because we are enjoying this kind of love, we are not trying to mold or change each other according to our own expectations or views. We are just receiving one another in this life and enjoying this life together, and the issue is a love that is expressed in the church. It is the very divine nature embodied in us and among us. The Lord said, "By this all will know that you are My disciples, if you have love for one another" (John 13:35). This love is not our conditional love but the unconditional flow of God's love between us.

Why is it so utterly important for us to know the vertical love relationship with the Lord that dispenses life into our being? It is because this vertical love relationship ushers us into the horizontal relationship in which we are gathered together under one Head. Then He and we just say, "My people" and "mercy." Hallelujah! It is all mercy. Oh, may the Lord grant us to see the extent of this marvelous unconditional love that reaches every kind of condition and brings us first to His life and then to the church. We love to say "church life," because Christ loved the church and gave Himself up for her!

Christ loved the church when she was a Gomer. He gave Himself up for her. When He loved her and died for her, she was not a perfected bride. She was a harlot, a Gomer, but He loved her. He loved her with all her blemishes and all her spots and all her corruption. He loved her and gave Himself for her. That is the love of God. He loves the church. He took a "mass of corruption" and He loved her, and gave Himself up for her, that [26] "He might sanctify and cleanse her with the washing of water by the word, [27] that He might present her to Himself a glorious church, not having spot or wrinkle or any such thing, but that she should be holy and without blemish" (Eph. 5:26-27).

By a lot of speaking — a lot of washing of water in the word — by a lot of cleansing, the spots are being removed. There are many things being washed continuously among us. The glorious church is based upon Christ's work and His righteousness and all that He has done. Praise the Lord for this wonderful love! This love issues in life and the building of the church. God's economy takes place in this unconditional love.

4

Manifestations of God's Unconditional Love

In the book of Hosea we have an unveiling of what God's love is really like. And the way the Lord unveils His love is by telling Hosea to go marry a wife of harlotry, a woman whose name is Gomer. Gomer symbolizes the *nature* of those God's love pursued — failing, corrupt, spoiled humanity. Hosea taking Gomer for his wife demonstrates the *nature* of God's love toward us.

Hosea's name means "salvation." Thus, when Hosea married Gomer, *salvation* married *failure*. This was God's design — that salvation would love failure and deliver her. These two were joined to demonstrate the nature of God's love. Gomer, the unfaithful wife whose affections were in another direction, was continuously loved by her faithful husband, Hosea. The Lord likened Hosea's love toward Gomer to His love toward Israel.

Gomer did not meet any condition to deserve Hosea's love. She did quite the opposite. Humanly speaking, she disqualified herself from being an object of her husband's love. In the same way, we would think we have disqualified ourselves from being an object of God's love. After all, we are nothing but Gomers. We are spoiled by sin, the flesh, and the devil. Yet God loves us and demonstrates that love. Romans 5:8 says,

"God demonstrates His own love toward us, in that while we were still sinners" — while we were Gomers — "Christ died for us." We have become the objects of the love of God. Not only as sinners are we the objects of His love, but also as believers. Even after we have received Christ, we may have a deep-rooted backsliding record — yet we are still the objects of His love. As a believer, having a history full of failure causes us to feel somewhat alienated from the Lord. We may have taken a thought that we are "out of the race" because of so much failure. We conclude that God's love surely has to be diminished in our case. But the book of Hosea shows us that God's unconditional love is not diminished by any kind of failure; rather, His love continues to be solid and dependable. You can count on it. Even now, right in your condition, God's love is staring you in the face.

We have seen the evil, corrupt condition of the objects of God's love and how much His love touches the uttermost negative condition. We are the objects of God's love because we have been put in Christ. We are locked up with Him. God involved us with Himself and we cannot get uninvolved. We may make a decision to give Him up, but He will never make a decision to give us up. In John 10:28 the Lord says, "And I give them eternal life, and they shall never perish." His seed remains in us (1 John 3:9). We are born of God and we cannot get unborn. We were begotten of the Father (1 Pet. 1:3), so we have His life.

Regardless of our condition, we are involved with His Son, and the Son is the object of the Father's love. Thus, wherever we go, we take Jesus with us. If we go into the mudhole, we take Christ into the mud with us. He goes with us because He is inside of us. He is there all the time in His unconditional love. So we can see the extent of God's love. Even if we make our bed in hell, His love will reach us there (Psa. 139:8).

Relationship-changing love

Let us look at the manifestations of God's unconditional love in the book of Hosea. These manifestations are detailed throughout the book. In chapter 2 we see the manifestation of His love. Hosea 2:16 says, "And it shall be, in that day, says the LORD, that you will call Me '*My Husband.*' " Literally in Hebrew this means "My Man." It is more endearing and intimate than saying "My Husband." To say "He is my Man" means that I am joined to this One.

Then in verse 17 the Lord says, "For I will take from her mouth the names of the Baals, and they shall be remembered by their name no more." The word *Baal* means "a lord" or "a ruler." It refers to a kind of tyranny over the people in their idolatry. *Baal* means that they had a relationship which was characterized by bondage, ruling, tyranny, and fear, rather than love. But when the Lord reaches them in their idolatry, He says, "In that day, you will call Me 'My Man' [or, 'My Husband']." This means that God's love is a relationship-changing love. He changes our entire relationship with Him from that of a ruler that we fear, to a husband who loves us and with whom we are enjoying a wonderful fellowship.

Or sometimes in our experience, our relationship with the Lord is characterized by fear as a result of being ruled in a wrong sense — in bondage under the law. Paul describes the law's ruling over us in Romans 7:1: "Or do you not know, brethren (for I speak to those who know the law), that the law has dominion [rules] over a man as long as he lives?" Then he speaks of being married to the law — that hard, ruling husband that brings us into bondage and activates sin even more.

At the same time, Paul tells us that as believers we are married to *Another,* "even to Him who was raised from the dead" (7:4). So we are joined to our resurrected Husband. Because He is now joined to our spirit, we are one spirit with Him (1 Cor. 6:17). Now, rather than being related to the law, we are related to a Person — our Lord Jesus Christ. And our relationship with the Lord is characterized by love, grace, mercy, and fellowship. In this kind of relationship with the Lord, we enjoy an ease in coming to Him. We can approach Him without timidity and fear. We are not thinking that maybe now God has a different attitude toward us. No, when the love of God comes to us and we see God's unconditional love, our whole relationship with the Lord is changed from fear to love. He brings us into this kind of enjoyment.

We have seen that one of the manifestations of God's unconditional love to His people is that they will call Him "My Man, My Husband." Then the Lord says in Hosea 2:17, "I will take from her mouth the names of the Baals, and they shall be remembered by their name no more." This indicates that in our relationship with the Lord in love, He will remove all remembrance of being under bondage to the law. Our relationship with Him will be altogether characterized by intimacy and love. Relating to Him in any other way will not even come to our thought. This shows us that the unconditional love of God radically changes our relationship with the Lord.

Some of us need this radical change in our relationship with the Lord because we base God's love toward us absolutely on how we feel and on our record of failures or successes. We imagine that God either loves us or does not love us according to whether or not we have had "a good day" or "a good week." But Hosea reveals that God's love is unmistakably unconditional.

In Jeremiah 31:3 the Lord says to Israel, "I have loved you with an everlasting love." And in Ezekiel 16, He tells her that He saw her in her nativity, on the day she was born. In verse 6 He says, "And when I passed by you and saw you struggling in your own blood, I said to you in your blood, Live! Yes, I said to you in your blood, Live!" And He made them alive and caused them to thrive and mature, and He shepherded them.

This was their condition — they were in their blood. This means they were wallowing in their misery, in their death. And He said, "I saw you." He found them in their blood. Has He ever caught you in that condition? One day you were in your blood, wallowing in your misery and your failure. When you deserved a spanking, God said, "I love you. I demonstrated it. Your sins are on My Son. He bore them once and for all. Now just come to Me. Come and be loved." This is relationship-changing love.

Healing love

Let us see more of the manifestations of God's unconditional love in Hosea 6. Verses 1-3 say, [1] "Come, and let us return to the LORD; for He has torn, but He will heal us; He has stricken, but He will bind us up. [2] After two days He will revive us; on the third day He will raise us up, that we may live in His sight. [3] Let us know, let us pursue the knowledge of the LORD. His going forth is established as the morning; He will come to us like the rain, like the latter and former rain to the earth." This is the way the Lord's love is manifested to us.

These verses in Hosea 6 are based upon Deuteronomy 32:39, where the Lord spoke through Moses saying, "Now see that I, even I, am He, and there is no God besides Me; I kill and I make alive; I wound and I heal; nor is there any who can deliver from My hand." This is a revelation of God's sovereignty over us: "I kill and I make alive. I wound and I heal." He is involved in all of it. He heals, binds up, revives, and raises us up, that we may live in His sight. All this signifies healing love.

Love in the realm of resurrection

God's sovereign love has a pattern in all of our experiences — the pattern of death and resurrection. This pattern begins with our going into death and passing through death, where our natural life is tested. The testing has the effect of wounding, striking, and ultimately weakening our natural strength. Passing through these environments we are "delivered to death," as Paul describes in 2 Corinthians 4:11. In these situations we have little feeling or sensation of God. It is a kind of death. This is a part of the pattern of God's sovereign love. Then the Lord revives us, and on the third day He raises us up in order that we may experience life out of death. This is another part of the pattern of His sovereign love — resurrection life out of death. "He has torn, but He will heal us; He has stricken, but He will bind us up." This means that He will bring us forth in resurrection.

Sovereign love

God's unconditional love is a sovereign love. This sovereign love embraces the totality of our living — all our *inward* circumstances, such as how we feel, how we react, and how we relate, as well as all our *outward* circumstances, which are things that happen to us that cause us to react. God is wonderfully sovereign in His ways over us. He knows how our heart is prone to wander from Him. Because He knows exactly where our heart is at any given moment, He allows circumstances that affect the condition of our heart (Rom. 8:26-28). Thus, like Paul in Romans 9:20, we simply need to come under the sovereign love of God: "But indeed, O man, who are you to reply against God? Will the thing formed say to him who formed it, Why have you made me like this?" Who can say to the Potter, "Why have You made me like this?" In other words, who can say, "Why did this happen to me?"

Paul continues to challenge our reasoning mind in Romans 9:21: "Does not the potter have power over the clay?" It is the Potter's choice to fashion this lump of clay in whatever way He desires. And if the clay is marred in His hand, He takes it off the potter's wheel and reshapes it again, as it seems good to Him. Praise the Lord, our lives are altogether under His sovereignty.

Who can add one cubit to his stature? (Matt. 6:27). Who can control tomorrow? Who can predict what will happen next week? (James 4:13-15). We are under God's sovereign, unconditional love. In Deuteronomy 33:27, He assures us that He is carrying us in His arms: "The eternal God is your refuge, and underneath are the everlasting arms." His arms are underneath us. Thus, if we are torn, if we are stricken, that is part of the process of death and resurrection, in order that the life of Christ might be exhibited in us and through us.

In 2 Corinthians 4:11 Paul says, "For we who live are always delivered to death for Jesus' sake, that the life of Jesus also may be manifested in our mortal flesh." Here the phrase "for Jesus' sake" should be literally translated "because of Jesus." It is because of Jesus that we are handed over to environments of perplexity and confusion. The word "perplexed" used by Paul in verse 8 of this passage comes from the Greek word *aporeo* (ἀπορέω). The prefix means "no," and the root means "way." Thus, it is rendered "no way" or "at a loss for a way." We have no way. We have no answers.

Many times God, in His sovereign love, designs that you have no answer. You are in front of a wall. You cannot go over it, around it, or under it. There is no way that you can penetrate it. There is no answer. You just kneel in front of the wall and say, "Lord Jesus, thank You I'm in Your hands." In this kind of death situation — whatever it is — He will revive you. And on the third day, He will raise you up in resurrection. This means that God needs a little time to prove that it is not you delivering yourself. After a few days there in death, you begin to "stink." You begin to realize there is no ability in you. But then, seemingly out of nowhere, there is an inner surge, an inner welling up of life. Then your mind begins to see things differently. You see that God is sovereign over all. He has torn and He is going to heal. He is healing you now. He has stricken you and He will bandage you up.

Thus, God's sovereign love comes to us in a pattern: death and resurrection, death and resurrection. This cycle is repeated over and over again in our experience. Just as the Lord Jesus passed through death and resurrection, we follow in His pattern. This is how Paul wanted to know the Lord. And Hosea 6:1-3 also speaks of our following on to know the Lord. Do you want to know the Lord? The way to know the Lord is to know Him in death and resurrection. In Philippians 3:10-11 Paul said, [10] "That I may know Him and the power of His resurrection, and the fellowship of His sufferings, being conformed to His death, [11] if, by any means, I may attain to the resurrection from the dead." This is how we know the Lord, not according to our thought but according to His thought — through death and resurrection.

You may want to shout from the mountaintops, "Hallelujah for His sovereign love!" The period of death that you are passing through may be a little longer than you would have expected. But, oh, the resurrection — the life coming out of death, which expresses Him. This is the unconditional love of God. It is God's sovereign love as well as His love in the realm of resurrection.

Handling love

Hosea 11:2 says, "As they called them so they went from them." This means that God's speaking came through the prophets to His people, Israel, but they ran from His speaking. Verse 2 continues, "They sacrificed to the Baals, and burned incense to carved images." This shows that God's people continued in their rebellion. Then in verses 3-4 God says, ³ "I taught Ephraim to walk, taking them by their arms; but they did not know that I healed them. ⁴ I drew them with gentle cords, with bands of love, and I was to them as those who take the yoke from their neck. I stooped and fed them." These verses describe God's handling love. It is the way He handles us in our rebellion.

Here in Hosea 11:2 there is rebellion. God sent His servants to His people, and the people turned away from them. They went back to their Baals and they sacrificed to them. Do you know what God's unconditional love does when His people are in that state? He says, "I taught Ephraim to walk, taking them by their arms; but they did not know that I healed them." This describes the tenderness with which the Lord handled His people. Then in verse 4 He further explains how He handled them: "I drew them with gentle cords, with bands of love." "Gentle cords" and "bands of love" are in apposition to one another, that is, the gentle cords are the bands of love.

In these verses Ephraim is pictured as a stubborn, rebellious heifer. Usually, stubborn heifers would be handled with thick ropes to control their rebellion. But God does not do that with us. He does not throw those heavy ropes over our rebellion and try to force us to the ground, and then draw us like a beast. He does not handle us that way. Even when we are rebellious, He is so delicate and so gentle. He draws us with gentle cords — cords of a man, not cords of a beast. Using thin gentle cords, He tugs slightly and draws until our rebellion begins to be subdued.

This is the way He handles us. In our rebellion and stubbornness, we may even try at times to get away from the Lord. Yet He does not subdue us by outward force. But He comes gently and draws us with bands of love, melting our heart. There is a song we enjoy singing about how the Lord, in His preciousness, subdues our stubborn will:

> Dear Lord Jesus, precious Jesus,
> How can I still stubborn be?
> At Thy feet cast all my hard'nings,
> And return with songs and singings;
> 'Tis my love to be Thy bondslave,
> *'Tis my joy to Thee obey.*

How can we be stubborn any longer, when His love overwhelms us and draws us? This is God's handling love.

Some years ago I was burdened for a person who was not making progress in the Lord. They were rebellious, and steeped in their rebellion. So I prayed with this verse every morning: "The kindness of God leads you to repentance" (Rom. 2:4). I prayed, "Lord, by Your kindness lead this one to repentance." And then I watched what happened in their environment — how God came, not in a direct way, but indirectly, in a way that caught their attention and won their interest. So God came to them, mellowed them, and broke them, drawing them with His kindness.

This is more of God's hedging-up love and His walling-in love. When you find yourself going after other loves, you need to pray, "Lord, hedge me up with a path of thorns and wall me in. Lord, grant Your kindness to lead me to repentance." Oh, God is so tender. His love is so thoughtful. He knows just how to handle us and how to touch the right place in our heart.

When I was a young man in high school, I was consumed with the dream of playing professional football. I was going my way and I had my goal. I was not seeking God. But I walked into a classroom in my sophomore year and saw a girl sitting on the front row. She really caught my attention. Little did I know that at that moment God was drawing me with cords of love. He was coming to me through what He knew would be meaningful to me and would attract me.

Through that young girl, who later became my wife, I found the Lord in my senior year. I knew He was real. Then He came and handled me in such a wonderful way. I had played varsity baseball for three years, but I had never had a high batting average. But when I found the Lord, something amazing happened. The sky was bluer, the grass was greener. I heard the birds singing. Confidence filled me. God was alive. I got up to the plate and hit nine straight singles in a row. This was all God's way of drawing me with cords of love. He came to me in my little concepts and views — in my little world — and made Himself so real.

This is God's delicate way of handling us. It is just like how a mother handles her naughty child. She knows that the child is naughty, but she also knows his disposition is of such a nature that if she reprimands him too strongly, he will lose heart and his whole being will inwardly give up. A wise mother will evaluate how to deal with the child's naughtiness, handling him according to his capacity to hear and receive.

This is how God's love came to rebellious Israel, who was like a kicking, stubborn heifer. Instead of throwing a noose around her neck with a big rope and forcing her to the ground, He drew her gently, tugging with strings of love. This is the love of God in Christ Jesus through the Holy Spirit, touching us and being manifested to us. He even touches our hearts through His love coming from others. Oh, this is precious. This is God's handling love.

Relieving love

Now let us enjoy another aspect of God's love in Hosea 11:4: "And I was to them as those who take the yoke from their neck. I stooped and fed them." Israel is pictured here as an animal under a heavy yoke. Then the Lord comes and takes the yoke from her neck. And because she had been in that position, under that kind of yoke for so long, He did not tell her to stand up erect to be fed. Instead, with one hand He took the yoke off; and with the other hand, He stooped down and fed her. This is God's relieving love. He takes the yoke off and He stoops and He feeds us.

Intrinsic and sympathetic love

Hosea 11:7-9 shows us yet more of God's heart of love toward us. Verse 7 says, "My people are bent on backsliding from Me. Though they call to the Most High, none at all exalt Him." In other words, they mouth the words, but they do not mean what they say. They do not really exalt Him. They are bent on backsliding. Then the Lord says in verse 8, "How can I give you up, Ephraim? How can I hand you over, Israel? How can I make you like Admah? How can I set you like Zeboiim?" As we mentioned earlier, these two cities are associated negatively with Sodom and Gomorrah in Deuteronomy 29:23. When God destroyed Sodom and Gomorrah, He included Admah and Zeboiim. So here He is saying to Israel, "How can I do that to you?"

In a sense, judicially, we deserve that kind of judgment because of our rebellion. But listen to God's intrinsic love, the love that is part of His very being. He is talking in a way that tells us He cannot help Himself. He loves us. But you ask, "Why?" There is no reason. It is electing love. It is because God chose to love you. God decided to make you an object of His love. So regardless of where you are — in blood, in death, in rebellion, in sin, in the world — you are an object of the love of God, you are a victim of that love. And one day you will come face to face with the fact that God loves you. Indeed, God's love and God's heart churns within Him. His sympathy is stirred over us. This is the kind of love God has toward His rebellious people.

A New Testament counterpart of Hosea 11:8 is Hebrews 4:14-16: [14] "Seeing then that we have a great High Priest who has passed through the heavens, Jesus the Son of God, let us hold fast our confession. [15] For we do not have a High Priest who cannot sympathize with our weaknesses, but was in all points tempted as we are, yet without sin. [16] Let us therefore come boldly to the throne of grace, that we may obtain mercy and find grace to help in time of need." The Lord is able to sympathize with our weaknesses. This reveals more of His intrinsic love. This sympathetic love comes from the One who has been tried and tempted in all points as we are.

The perfect tense is used in verse 15 for the word "tempted" or "tried." In the Greek language the perfect tense describes something that happened at a point of time in the past and has a continuing effect in the present. So the perfect tense defines a present state or reality that is based upon a past action. Thus the Lord as our High Priest is able to sympathize with our weaknesses as One who "was in all points tempted as we are" and *continues* to know and feel the pressures and agonies that we pass through in being tempted. He passed through it. He was tempted in all points yet without sin. It is not that He was tried two thousand years ago and now He no longer feels the effects of what He passed through. He knows presently all the pressures and the problems that we sinful human beings pass through in our trials. And He is able to sympathize with us in our weaknesses.

The Lord is not just there on the throne objectively looking at us from afar. Because He lives in us, He is sympathizing in and with our own weaknesses. He feels them. His sympathetic love is within us because He Himself has been tried. He was tempted in His will. He was tempted in His mind. He was tempted in His emotions. He was tempted in His body. He was tempted in every point. He knows the struggle. He knows the pressures. He knows it all. He still feels it this moment. On the throne, the One who has been tried continues presently to feel with us what we are passing through. He is fully entering into our feelings — feeling our feelings with us, bearing what we bear. His sympathy is not merely an outward advising or instructing like we might receive from a counselor in the world. The Lord as our Counselor has a way, from within us, of feeling and sympathizing with our weaknesses. This is the kind of love expressed in Hosea. This is intrinsically how the Lord feels toward us.

Death- and grave-conquering love

Now let us look at Hosea 13:14: "I will ransom them from the power of the grave; I will redeem them from death. O Death, I will be your plagues! O Grave, I will be your destruction!" This verse is quoted by Paul in 1 Corinthians 15:55. Revealed here is what we could call death- and grave-conquering love. Praise the Lord, because of His resurrection, we no longer fear death. The Lord says that He will ransom His people "from the power of the grave" and redeem them "from death." Then He speaks directly to death and the grave, personifying them. To death He is saying, "O Death, you have exercised tyranny over mankind. Everyone fears death. But, O Death, do you know what I am going to do? I am going to plague you by passing through you and coming out in resurrection." "O Death, I will be your plagues! O Grave, I will be your destruction." Death and the grave have swallowed up much, but now our Lord has destroyed both. Now the resurrected Christ is our Hope!

All of us one day are appointed to die. We will die. But we can say, "O Death, O Grave, because my Christ has destroyed you, I will be raised incorruptible in a fresh, resurrected body that is being kept for me right now" (2 Cor. 5:1-2). We will receive a new body, redeemed from the power of the grave. And all believers will be together in resurrected bodies just as the Lord Jesus is. We are going to have a glorious meeting in the air with a universal gathering on Mount Zion, with an innumerable company of angels (Heb. 12:22).

This death-conquering love has redeemed us from the power of the grave. It conquers death and it conquers the grave, giving us a living hope (1 Pet. 1:3). With this hope Paul comforted the Thessalonian believers concerning their loved ones who had "fallen asleep." He did not want them to sorrow as others "who have no hope" (1 Thess. 4:13-18). We do not mourn like the world, because this life on earth is just temporary. We are merely sojourners here, awaiting our entrance into the manifestation of the kingdom in resurrection.

Accommodating love

Finally, in Hosea 14:1-3 the Lord gives us a practical way to respond to His unconditional love. He is so accommodating that, after all the rebellion throughout the book of Hosea, He pursues with His love to the end — until it accomplishes His goal. As a teacher would instruct a small child, He says to His people in verse 1, "O Israel, return to the LORD your God, for you have stumbled because of your iniquity." Then, putting their history of failure behind them, He tells them how to return to Him in verse 2: "Take words with you, and return to the LORD." And He even tells them what to say: "Say to Him, Take away all iniquity." Just say, "Lord, take it away." And then He tells them to say, "Receive us graciously." This means "Receive us in grace, for good." Then He further releases them from their load of guilt by telling them what to offer: "For we will offer the sacrifices of our lips." He does not tell them to perform rituals and offer many different sacrifices. Nor does He require them to bring gold and silver as gifts, as they had done in worshiping their idols. The Lord just has them use their mouth: "Take words with you."

This principle of using our mouth to confess is presented again in Romans 10:6-9: [6] "Do not say in your heart, 'Who will ascend into heaven?' (that is, to bring Christ down from above) [7] or, 'Who will descend into the abyss?' (that is, to bring Christ up from the dead). [8] But what does it say? 'The word is near you, even in your mouth and in your heart' . . . [9] that if you confess with your mouth the Lord Jesus . . . you will be saved."

How do we return to the Lord? Just take words. Just use your mouth. Do not do anything but come with words. What words? Words like "Thank You, Lord. Take away my sin." That is all. In Luke 18 the tax collector praying in the temple used these kinds of words. Verse 13 says, "And the tax collector, standing afar off, would not so much as raise his eyes to heaven, but beat his breast, saying, God be merciful to me a sinner!" He did not even lift up his head. He just said "God!" Beating on his breast, he said, "God be merciful to me a sinner!" He just took words. And verse 14 tells us, "This man went down to his house justified." He had simply offered the sacrifice of lips. Lips! This is always the way to respond to God's love. It is simply to say "Jesus, thank You for the blood. Thank You for Your love." Just return to Him.

This is His accommodating love — He makes full provision for us to return to Him. This is the way He touches us, drawing us completely back to Himself. The best words you can take to the Lord are "Lord Jesus." In that name is a healing balm. In that name we enjoy the fellowship of that Person, because the name means His person. To call His name is to offer the sacrifice of praise with our lips, which Paul entreats us to do in Hebrews 13:15: "Therefore by Him let us continually offer the sacrifice of praise to God, that is, the fruit of our lips, giving thanks to His name." Let us take words and return to the Lord.

The ultimate effect of the Lord's accommodating love toward us is seen in Hosea 14:8: "Ephraim shall say, 'What have I to do anymore with idols?' And the Lord says to Ephraim, "I have heard and observed him. I am like a green cypress tree; your fruit is found in Me." Here we see that God's unconditional love toward us in all our rebellion has the effect of fully reducing us to Himself.

What a blessed day when in one situation after another we are just reduced to God Himself — "Your fruit is found in

Me." Are you anxious? Your answer, your way, is found in Him. Just call His name. Keep touching Him. Keep enjoying Him! Are you pressed, tried, tempted? Your fruit now is found in Him. Just stay with Him. Abide in His love. Stay in His love and He will dispense His life power into your being (Luke 8:43-48).

This is how we go on with the Lord — by just taking some words and being reduced to Him. Love Him, enjoy Him, and enjoy this unconditional love that has been manifested to us. We have the sense that His fingerprints of love are all over us. He has said it all. He has done it all. Now we just need to return. Wherever your heart is, wherever you have traveled, you can return. Return and take some words with you. Maybe your words are just "Mercy, Lord." Or maybe your words are "Give me understanding, Lord." Or maybe your words are "Lord, take my sins away." Whatever, just take some words and speak them quietly to the Lord and be joyfully reduced to Him.

5

Capturing Love

God's love replacing our idols

The summation of the whole book of Hosea is expressed in verse 8 of chapter 14: "Ephraim shall say, What have I to do anymore with idols?" This phrase, out of the mouth of Ephraim, indicates that he had been joined to idols; he had been far away from the Lord. Yet now something has affected him to the point that he utters this question, "What have I to do anymore with idols?" This is a voluntary expression — an expression of freedom and choice. It is uttered because Ephraim has found something much more desirable, much more beautiful, than the idols that had so attracted him. He has now come to a point where he is ready to drop everything related to idols. These are his own words.

Then in the next phrase God is speaking. He says, "I have heard and observed him." This indicates that as the utterance came out of Ephraim's mouth, "What have I to do anymore with idols?" the Lord heard it and observed him. Then Ephraim speaks again, describing himself: "I am like a green cypress tree." This denotes fruitfulness from a spontaneous flow of life. Then God replies in the last part of verse 8, "Your fruit is found in Me," showing that Ephraim was reduced solely to God Himself.

Everyone knows that rather than beating off dead leaves from the branches of a tree, you simply allow the sap with its new life to flow up from the trunk out through the branches. The new life will spontaneously cause all the dead leaves to fall off. It is as if to say, "Whatever idols I was joined to, they have fallen away, because the new, fresh sap of God and the love of God is flowing." What is new and living pushes out everything old and dead — everything that is not God. This is what the capturing love of God does — it causes us to have nothing to do anymore with idols.

This kind of response from Ephraim, "What have I to do anymore with idols?" sounds like something a spiritual person would say. The words come from a person whose heart has been so affected, so taken over. It was not a takeover due to being under a mandate or command to "love not the world." This heart was taken over by another love that caused the love of the world to fade away. This is what happens to our heart.

Let me illustrate. When I was a boy, I loved to play with soldiers, sandbags, and airplanes. I could spend hours on the floor, setting up the soldiers and tanks. Then I would add my own sound effects to make it all the more real to me. That was the world I loved. But then as I grew older, something happened to me. I just didn't care for those things anymore. I found myself in another realm — I loved football, basketball, and baseball. I was occupied with a new love. The other love had faded away. Something else replaced it.

This is exactly what Ephraim experienced. His heart was riveted to so many other things. But God's love came, and that new love and relationship with the Lord replaced everything else. So Ephraim could utter a statement like this: "What have I to do anymore with idols?"

God's ignoring love

Let us return to Hosea 4 and see Ephraim in his past. Verses 17-18 say, "Ephraim is joined to idols, let him alone." Because Ephraim represents, in a sense, the whole northern kingdom of Israel, we could say that what is described here in verses 17 and 18 is the condition of Israel: [17] "Ephraim is joined to idols, let him alone. [18] Their drink is rebellion, they commit harlotry continually. Her rulers dearly love dishonor."

At this point, God's love was manifested to Ephraim in a way of just leaving him to himself, to become, as it were, completely nauseated with his idols. Eventually, this ignoring love of God would cause Ephraim to voluntarily, on his own, come back to say, "What have I to do anymore with idols?" This is the effect of God's ignoring love.

God's unchanging love

Hosea 7:8 says, "Ephraim has mixed himself among the peoples; Ephraim is a cake unturned." Here the condition of Ephraim is described not only as being idolatrous, but also as mingling himself among the pagan lifestyles and practices of the nations. Instead of walking as a people separated unto God, Ephraim had actually mixed himself with the pagans and their idolatry. The end result was that he departed from the

Lord. The description of Ephraim as "a cake unturned" indicates that God was coming to judge Ephraim in a disciplinary way. But Ephraim did not recognize or pay any attention to God's sovereign dealings in his environment. Thus, even when the judgment came, with the divine intention of dealing with him for his profit, he remained, as it were, a cake unturned. This means that he was spoiled.

In the ancient world, when baking a cake you had to turn it over again and again every few minutes. In this way, it could be evenly baked. But Ephraim was a cake unturned, indicating that he was burned completely on one side and was therefore ruined. They were a spoiled, ruined group of people because all God's dealings in their life were wasted. They did not turn. They were not affected. They did not repent. They were continually backsliding, and God lovingly came in His judgments to discipline them. He came to affect them, to cause them to turn; but they did not turn. So God likens them to a cake unturned — a spoiled cake.

Sometimes in our experience, we have been like Ephraim. God has tried over and over again to get through in our life, yet we have resisted Him again and again. He has come in different ways by His providence in our environments. He came to affect us by hedging up our way with thorns. He made things difficult for us when we were going after our other lovers and pursuing our own fleshly way. Deep inside we knew the Lord was causing us trouble because we were pursuing a course that absolutely departed from Him. But we closed our ears to His speaking, to the Spirit within us. As a result we spoiled all His dealings. None of them worked for good (Heb. 12:5-13). So Ephraim remained "a cake unturned" — burned, ruined, spoiled; and he had "mixed himself among the peoples." This is the condition of Ephraim that eventually led him to the stage of saying, "What have I to do anymore with idols?"

Your condition may be like Ephraim's, and you may feel that there is no way for the Lord's love to reach you in your hardness and in your history of rejecting His dealings. If so, just take a long look at the book of Hosea to see the depths of the love of God toward you. God's unchanging love kept pursuing Ephraim. When Ephraim joined himself to idols, God's love was there. When Ephraim spoiled God's providential dealings that He lovingly measured out, God's love was there. This is Ephraim, and this is God's unconditional love.

God's churning love

Let us look now at Hosea 8:11-12. Here the Lord says, [11] "Because Ephraim has made many altars for sin, they have become for him altars for sinning. [12] I have written for him the great things of My law, but they were considered a strange thing." This means Ephraim rejected God's word about having one altar and one place of worship — Jerusalem. They left the truth, they left the Word of God, and they left the one altar at which all of God's people were to worship. They set up for themselves altars in the north, and those became altars for sinning.

Ephraim was practicing organized sin in the northern kingdom similar to "organized crime." Sin was not just an occasional happening there. Their whole organized system of worship and idolatry was what the Lord called "altars for sinning." They were taking substitutes for the reality of the living God.

Then Hosea 11:12 says, "Ephraim has encompassed Me with lies, and the house of Israel with deceit." This is more of Ephraim's condition. He is joined to idols, he is a cake unturned, he has rejected the word of the Lord, and he is full of lies. Then look at God's feeling about this very object of His love. Hosea 11:8 says, "How can I give you up, Ephraim? How can I hand you over, Israel? How can I make you like Admah? How can I set you like Zeboiim?" These two cities were overthrown with Sodom and Gomorrah. The Lord mentions them here to reveal to Ephraim that his condition and what he had done was worthy to be treated as Sodom and Gomorrah.

But here we see the intrinsic revelation of God's love. His very Being is expressed in His speaking: "How can I give you up, Ephraim?" This is like God speaking to you. Maybe you feel like you have been joined to idols. You have spoiled God's discipline in your life. You have resisted Him. You feel like a cake unturned. You have even taken the devil's categorizing — that you are just a spoiled piece of humanity, that you have sinned yourself to ruin. Maybe all of this is how you feel. But over and above your feeling is God's revelation of His love to you. And He is saying, "How can I give you up?" In other words, God's love goes beyond Ephraim being joined to idols, being a cake unturned, rejecting the Word of God, and being full of lies and deceit.

Then the Lord continues in Hosea 11:8, "My heart churns within Me; My sympathy is stirred." Here God's love is revealed as something intrinsic to His very Being. You cannot take it out of Him. This is His churning love. On the one hand, Ephraim deserves every kind of judgment for his absolute, willful rebellion against God. His awful record merits him being cast off completely. Yet, when God's judgment comes to the foreground, mercy prevails and love overcomes Him. Far more than the consideration of any kind of judgment, love and mercy prevail.

"My heart churns within Me" means that there is a turning within God Himself. This turning within God's heart is also seen in Genesis 18:16-32 when Abraham prayed for Sodom: "Suppose there were fifty righteous within the city? . . . Suppose there should be forty righteous found there? . . . Suppose ten righteous should be found there? . . ." Abraham appealed to the Lord in this way when He was about to destroy Sodom. Abraham's prayer could actually turn God and re-mind Him of His mercy and His love; and that is what prevailed—His churning heart of love. This is the love of God unveiled in Hosea 11:8. He says, "My sympathy is stirred."

As a result of His love, God says in verse 9, "I will not execute the fierceness of My anger; I will not again destroy Ephraim. For I am God, and not man, the Holy One in your midst; and I will not come with terror." Here we see that in God's heart He considers His love toward us to be a very weighty factor in our relationship with Him. We have to consider this when we are talking to the Lord. Consider how much He loves you and how much you mean to Him. Such consideration is based upon the Word of God.

God's choosing love

Let us look more at this loving consideration in the heart of God. Deuteronomy 7:6 says, "For you are a holy people to the LORD your God; the LORD your God has chosen you to be a people for Himself, a special treasure above all the peoples on the face of the earth." To God, there is something so special about the corporate entity of the Body of Christ, which includes Israel in the Old Testament and the church in the New Testament. God's heart-attitude continues to be expressed in verses 7-9, [7] "The LORD did not set His love on you nor choose you because you were more in number than any other people, for you were the least of all peoples; [8] but because the LORD loves you, and because He would keep the oath which He swore to your fathers, the LORD has brought you out with a mighty hand, and redeemed you from the house of bondage, from the hand of Pharaoh king of Egypt. [9] Therefore know that the LORD your God, He is God, the faithful God who keeps covenant and mercy for a thousand generations with those who love Him and keep His commandments."

Verse 7 tells us that the Lord did not set His love on us or choose us because we were "more in number." This conveys the thought that the Lord did not love us or choose us because of anything intrinsically in ourselves — not because of our righteousness, not because of our condition, not because we have done anything, but simply because the Lord loves us. Why the Lord set His love on us and why the Lord says, "Jacob I have loved and Esau I have hated" — why God loves Jacob, when Jacob was what he was — we will never know. It is simply God's sovereign, unequivocal love. Thus, our relationship with the Lord is not based on anything that we are, but exclusively on Him loving us. We were chosen in Him before the foundation of the world to be the objects of His love (Eph. 1:4, 6).

So when we come to the Lord, we need to come to Him with all our unworthiness and tell Him about His love, His mercy, His compassion, and His sympathy. This so easily stirs up His heart because we are touching His love that has been demonstrated at the cross for sinners. It is our enjoyment of that poured-out love that stirs up God's heart toward us. We, like Jacob and Ephraim, are the objects of God's unequivocal love.

As we continue through the book of Hosea with all the descriptions of the condition of God's people, we find several more references to Ephraim. For example, Hosea 13:12 further exposes his doings: "The iniquity of Ephraim is bound up; his sin is stored up." This indicates that there was an accumulation of sin in Ephraim's experience. Yet God's love was manifested in chapter 14, verse 4: "I will heal their backsliding, I will love them freely." And then in verse 8 Ephraim responds: "What have I to do anymore with idols?"

The dropping effect of God's love

It is wonderful that in our whole relationship with the Lord, with all our unworthiness, we can be transferred from fear, bondage, and threat to the security of the everlasting love that will bring us again and again to the Lord in fellowship and enjoyment. Being in this love causes us to drop every idol. It is possible in the Christian life to have a relationship with the Lord in which we can love Him more than any object that our emotion is riveted to this moment. You cannot imagine that you could be freed from a sinful, fleshly, inordinate affection. But there is a love — a love for God, a love for Jesus — that is stronger than any other love and any other cord tugging at our hearts. He can break every cord. So we just need to bask in His love and cultivate and enjoy it. Tell Him, "Lord, just reveal to me this capturing love, this love that captures even me."

This love is eternal in the Father. It was demonstrated by the Son. And now it is poured out in our hearts through the Holy Spirit. So this love was not left back in eternity past where God loved us, chose us, and predestinated us. Neither was it left back at the cross two thousand years ago when God demonstrated His love for us through the death of His Son. But now, that very love — out of eternity, through incarnation, through human living, through crucifixion, in resurrection — now that love is poured out in our hearts through the Holy Spirit who was given to us.

So the love of God today is a flow. This is why we praise and pray and exercise our spirit by speaking to one another (Eph. 5:18-21). We are drawing up from our innermost being this flowing love of God that has been poured out in our hearts by the Holy Spirit. The Holy Spirit is the conveyor of the affections of the love of God — affections that are riveted to God. Now these affections flow in the Spirit to become our affections and our enjoyment. This really captures us.

6

The Nature of God's Unconditional Love

One love in three directions

We need to see the nature of God's unconditional love because this love is the very essence of His relationship to us. And this love should be the very essence of our relationship to Him. It should also be the essence of our relationship to one another. God's love first comes to us and causes us to love Him; and in loving Him, we love one another. These three dimensions are the dimensions of the love of God — His love toward us, our love toward Him, and our love toward one another.

The nature of our love toward the Lord and toward one another should not be any different from His love toward us. The love that reaches us, and is poured out into our hearts by God, is the same love that returns back to Him in worship, praise, enjoyment, and intimate fellowship. It is also the same love that flows out from us to one another. It is altogether one love flowing in three directions — God's unconditional love coming from God to us, and then going back from us to God, and then horizontally going out to one another. This is one kind of love, not three different loves. There is not one kind of love that God has for us, then another kind of love that we have toward God, and then a third kind of love that we have toward one another. No, the *agape* love is one love; it is one essence. It has one nature and that nature flows in all directions. May we see more of the nature of that unconditional love so that we could have a proper and more accurate realization and experience of the love of God.

Love as the distinguishing characteristic of believers

Let us see this one love flowing out in all directions in John 13:34-35. Verse 34 says, "A new commandment I give to you, that you love one another, as I have loved you, that you also love one another." Here the Lord is speaking of a "new commandment." However, if you are familiar with the Old Testament, you know that the Lord had already given the commandment to love one another. In Leviticus 19:18 He says, "You shall love your neighbor as yourself."

But here in John 13:34 the Lord defines the nature of this new commandment and, in so doing, contrasts it to the old commandment that preceded it. He says, "Love one another, *as* I have loved you." This means that in the same, identical way that He loves us, we are to love one another. This is the nature of the new commandment — the kind of love we have toward one another is to be identical to the very love the Lord Jesus has for us.

Then the Lord adds in verse 35, "By this all will know that you are My disciples, if you have love for one another." Thus, the distinguishing characteristic of the believers, that is, of the Lord's disciples, is that we have love toward one another. What distinguishes the church, the Body of Christ, more than any other characteristic is that in our relationships we have love toward one another. "By this all will know" means that this is what is going to distinguish us and mark us out. This is what is going to speak to the world. This is what is going to speak louder than any sermon, any message, or any set of beliefs. What will speak louder to people around us is the love we have toward one another.

The "love for one another" in verse 35 is already defined in verse 34. It is the love with which He has loved us: "*As* I have loved you, that you also love one another." So this love is really one love. We enjoy this love as a sinner condemned, ungodly, and without anything to merit favor from God. In that condition, God, in an unconditional way, out of His free love, comes to us to save us. In mercy, He cleanses us, restores us, and reconciles us to Himself by His redemptive work (Titus 3:5 and 2 Cor. 5:18).

There are no words to describe this kind of love. It is God's redeeming love coming to a lost sinner who is, as Ezekiel expresses, lying there helpless in his own blood, not able to rise up, not able to do anything. In Ezekiel 16:6 the Lord says, "And when I passed by you and saw you struggling in your own blood, I said to you in your blood, 'Live!' Yes, I said to you in your blood, 'Live!'" There you were in the wilderness, by yourself, wallowing in your own blood; and He came to you, and He loved you, and He said to you, "Live!" This is God's love toward us.

The nature of this love of God that Ezekiel describes is the nature of the love that is to be among all believers, among all of God's children. The same love flowing from God to us flows from us to one another. Again, this is the distinguishing mark of the believers in Christ's Body, the church. This is how all men will know that we are the Lord's disciples.

The composition of God's unconditional love

Now let us look at the composition of God's unconditional love — what this love is made up of, what its very essence is. When we speak of God's unconditional love, we need to know that it is backed up by something. There are ingredients that make up this love, that give it its very nature.

God's choice and God's plan

First we will look at the nature of God's love in Ephesians 1:3-6. Verses 3-4 say, [3] "Blessed be the God and Father of our Lord Jesus Christ, who has blessed us with every spiritual blessing in the heavenly places in Christ, [4] just as He chose us in Him before the foundation of the world, that we should be holy and without blame before Him." Then the next phrase, "in love," can be included as part of verse 5, as some Bible versions translate it: [5] "In love, having predestined us unto sonship by Jesus Christ to Himself, according to the good pleasure of His will, [6] to the praise of the glory of His grace, by which He has graced us in the Beloved."

These marvelous verses show us the nature of God's unconditional love toward us. Part of what makes up that nature is His choice and His plan. It was wholly according to the good pleasure of His will that we were *chosen* in Him before the foundation of the world. This was before we were able to establish a history with God and make ourselves a little bit lovable to Him. It was before we could even set foot on the earth to demonstrate that we were a pretty good fellow so that God would maybe look at our sincerity and say, "I like that sincerity, so I am going to make you the object of My love." Before we even had a chance to try to demonstrate any qualities that would merit God's favor, He chose us in Christ before the foundation of the world. Thus His love in choosing us comes directly out of the good pleasure of His will.

Irrespective of what would happen in our life time — how many failures we would have, and what kind of history we would establish — irrespective of all of that, He chose us in Christ before the foundation of the world and eternally made us the object of His love. His love toward us comes from eternity past and goes to eternity future, passing through time, through the devil's work, through demonic activity, through failure, through sin, through the world, through guilt, through condemnation. This is God's love directed toward us out of eternity.

This love is based upon God's choice. Before Jacob was born, the word was uttered, "Jacob I have loved." Before Jacob and Esau were able to do anything good or bad, before they were out of Rebecca's womb, God said, "Jacob I have loved, but Esau I have hated" (Rom. 9:13). Don't try to understand this. You can't. God just says it, and in saying it He indicates that the essence of His love is altogether made up of His choice.

The fact that you are the object of God's love strongly testifies that you were chosen in Him before the foundation of the world. This is the nature of God's unconditional love. This is how He loves us — not dependent on conditions, but unconditionally — based upon the sheer good pleasure of His own will. You wonder why. We all wonder why. Yet we are not in the realm of getting an answer. We are in the realm of worship. We simply join with Paul in Romans 11:33-36 and exclaim, [33] "Oh, the depth of the riches both of the wisdom and knowledge of God! How unsearchable are His judgments and His ways past finding out! [34] For who has known the mind of the Lord? Or who has become His counselor? [35] Or who has first given to Him and it shall be repaid to him? [36] For of Him and through Him and to Him are all things, to whom be glory forever. Amen." This is the realm of praising and thanksgiving, the realm of "Thank You, Lord! I do not know why You chose me, but I thank You."

Have you ever received a gift and felt like you did not deserve it? You wondered why it was given to you. But the giver had no special reason. So all you could say was, "Thank you." Oh, this is the nature of God's love. It is based upon His choice and upon His plan.

God's plan is revealed in Ephesians 1:5, which says, "In love, having *predestined* us unto sonship by Jesus Christ to Himself." This shows us that we were marked out, set apart by God beforehand. Our destiny was determined prior to our birth. In love God predestined us unto His plan. And His plan is to conform us to the image of His firstborn Son. Christ's image is to be wrought into the very fibers of our being so that we would express Him and bear His image. This is what it means to be predestined unto sonship. It includes a full inward participation in the life of the Lord Jesus — from our spirit into our soul, and into our mortal body — so that Christ emanates from us. He just flows out of our being. We react like Him. We think like Him. Our attitudes are like Him. Our choices are His. He is our life. We are transformed into His image. As we bear the image of God's Son, we are fulfilling our predestination. This is all according to the good pleasure of God's will.

The nature, or essence, of God's love includes His choice and His plan. His choice is beyond our comprehension; but because He chose us, He set His love upon us. We have become the objects of His love and can only say with David, "Where can I flee from Your presence?" (Psa. 139:7). We cannot get away from God's love. It will find us out. It is the greatest hound that you will ever meet up with. Just as the police dogs sniff out things that are hidden, God's love will sniff us out. Regardless of where we are, even if we are buried under sin and condemnation, the love of God will come and find us there because we are the objects of that love.

This is the love of God toward us. And this is the same love we bear toward one another. This is the love in the church. We are not together because we each decided to join a group. We have assembled together with others who are also His chosen ones. We are with others who have a destiny over their life to be conformed to the image of God's Son. Who are we to receive or reject a member of the Body of Christ based upon our little rules? If a person has been born again, he is loved by the Lord. He is God's choice, and he is also one over whom

God's plan is being worked out. Thus, our part is only to acknowledge what God has done and receive him whom Christ has received. We are to "receive one another, just as Christ also received us, to the glory of God" (Rom. 15:7).

The love that chose me, predestined me, and reconciled me is the same love in our relationships with one another. So our relationships with one another have their source in eternity. It is not accidental that we are together. We are related to one another and we know one another as brothers and sisters. Our relatedness is based upon God's choice and His plan in eternity. Now, in time, we are with one another regardless of our condition, our background, our race — whatever. All those things mean nothing. God's love has been set over all of us; and now that love has been poured out in our heart, so we can simply let it flow toward one another.

Our relationships in the church are based upon an eternal love that chose us and predestined us unto sonship. Thus we are not related in a superficial, shallow way. We do not come together as a social gathering, merely saying hello and shaking each other's hand. We are related eternally in God's love and by His choice and plan.

When we as God's people rise up to see the essence and nature of this love between us, and begin relating to one another according to this love, "all will know" that we are the Lord's disciples (John 13:35). The world will know because this love is a defined love. It is the love of God's choice and the love of God's plan. And it issues in a distinguishing trait — we have love toward one another, even as Christ has loved us. So this passage in Ephesians reveals part of the composition, or nature, of God's unconditional love.

Christ's redemption

First, we have seen that God's love is made up of His choice and His plan. Second, we need to see that His unconditional love is made up of Christ's redemption. This is more of the essence of God's love. Romans 5:8 says, "But God demonstrates His own love toward us, in that while we were yet sinners, Christ died for us." This is Christ's redemption. With this verse in mind, let us look at Ephesians 5:25, which says, "Husbands, love your wives, just as Christ also loved the church and gave Himself for her." Paul is exhorting the husbands to love their wives in the same way that Christ loves the church.

Husbands and wives, you may be married to a Gomer — to a failure! Yet, did you know that when the Lord loved the church and gave Himself up for her, at that point she was not a perfected, glorious church? She was a Gomer. She was, as Ephesians 2 describes, "by nature children of wrath, just as the others." She was under the domination of the devil, living in the lust of the flesh and fulfilling its desires. She was all the things described in Ephesians 2:1-3. Yet this is what the Lord loved, as verse 4 says: "But God, who is rich in mercy, because of His great love with which He loved us..."

Often in a marriage the husband or wife lives with a concept about having "the ideal mate." What happens then is that he or she is loving an "ideal" person. In their courtship they had come to know each other in part, so their thought about one another was left in a realm of ideals. Then after some days of being married, all of a sudden the real person appears. So, there is the ideal thought over against the real situation. But when the Lord loved the church, He loved the raw material that needed to be cleansed and washed in the blood. He loved her when she was in a condition like Gomer's. And then He gave Himself for her.

This is redeeming love — that Christ died for us in our state of being ungodly and sinful. Thus, the unconditional love of God is made up of Christ's redemption. This is its essence. This makes God's love solid; it gives it substance. His love is not just a feeling He happens to have once in a while. God's unconditional love is steady and solid. It reaches back into eternity past and then manifests itself in time by God so loving the world that "He gave His only begotten Son" (John 3:16). His Son came and willingly offered His life for us. This is dying love. It is blood-shedding love. It is sin-bearing love. It is love that took our sin and our judgment. We can be pardoned and forgiven and made right with God because Jesus paid it all. This is the demonstration of God's love.

Love needs to be demonstrated. It is not enough just to say, "I love you," yet not demonstrate it. Even the Scripture indicates this: "God demonstrates His own love toward us, in that while we were yet sinners, Christ died for us." He proved His love. He manifested it. While we were Gomers, Christ died for us. This demonstrated, redeeming love is the essence of God's unconditional love.

Christ's resurrection and ascension

God's love is made up not only of His choice and plan and of Christ's redemption, but also of Christ's resurrection and ascension. Let us look now at this third aspect of His unconditional love. God's love has as its essence Christ's resurrecting power and ascending power. This is all part of the love. The love that God has toward us is not a detached love from the heavens that says, "I love you and I even died for you and you are forgiven." But it is a love that provides the very power to be changed. It imparts to us the very nature and life-power of resurrection to inwardly do the work over us sinful, fallen human beings. We have resurrection life in our spirit, joining us to the heavens in resurrection and ascension. So God's love is not limited in its abilities. It is not conditional love. It is unconditional because it is constituted with these elements — God's choice and His plan, Christ's death and redemption on the cross, and His resurrection with His ascension.

After seeing the detailed description of our sinful condition in Ephesians 2:1-3, let us look at verses 4-5: [4] "But God, who is rich in mercy, because of His great love with which He loved us, [5] even when we were dead in trespasses, made us alive together with Christ (by grace you have been saved)." These verses tell us not only that God is rich in mercy because of His great love with which He loved us, but they also tell us what this love did when we were dead. We did not have any life, but God "made us alive together with Christ." Then verse 6 tells us that God "raised us up together and made us sit together in the heavenly places in Christ Jesus."

Now this power of resurrection life has entered our spirit, joining us to the Lord who is a life-giving Spirit. He, this moment, is giving to us the resurrected, ascended life that He is living. In John 14:19 the Lord said, "Because I live, you will live also." He is alive in resurrection and ascension, and God has put everything under His feet (Heb. 2:8). Every demon is under His feet. He is the Lord of the universe! He has been crowned and He is sitting at God's right hand until all His enemies are made His footstool (Heb. 1:13). This resurrection power is His by authority. Because He died, the Father raised Him (Rom. 4:25). Now His life is available to enter into us. We are joined to this living One; and because He lives and we are joined to Him in our spirit, we will live also.

There is a life in our spirit that has power to change us. That life has become a drink to us. It has become our food. As we enjoy that life, it flows and it operates. It has the ability to tear down our hardness. It has the ability to work in us to actually change our choice, change our attitude, and change our feeling. That life in us can do a complete work on our insides because it has passed through human living and death itself. It has resurrected and ascended all the way to the throne, and now it has been dispensed into our spirit and is living, operating, and working in us.

All we need to do is stir up what is already within us. Second Timothy 1:6-7 says, [6] "Stir up [fan into flame] the gift of God which is in you.... [7] For God has not given us a spirit of fear, but of power and of love and of a sound mind." Resurrection power is in your spirit. You do not know the potential that is there. All you have to do is *fan into flame* the gift of God which is in you. The Greek verb literally means to "fire life up," to "fan" it. Fire up what is smoldering there. This means that you and I have a spirit that is joined to the resurrected, ascended Christ. And this resurrected, ascended One is just waiting for our spirits to be fanned. For example, when you come to a meeting of the church and you sing, pray, and praise, you are fanning. You are "firing life up," and then that life operates. Or during the day as you are going through some kind of trial, you just open yourself to call "Jesus." By speaking His name, you are fanning the flame, causing that resurrection life to operate and work. So the essence of God's unconditional love is made up of not only Christ's redemption but also His ever-present, operating resurrection and ascension power.

Christ's intercession

The fourth aspect of God's unconditional love is Christ's present intercession for us. The fact that there is Someone praying for us, interceding for us, is an expression of God's eternal love. In Romans 8:33-39 Paul confidently announces that Christ's intercession avails for us as part of God's unconditional love: [33] "Who shall bring a charge against God's elect? It is God who justifies. [34] Who is he who condemns? It is Christ who died, and furthermore is also risen, who is even at the right hand of God, who also makes intercession for us. [35] Who shall separate us from the love of Christ? Shall tribulation, or distress, or persecution, or famine, or nakedness, or peril, or sword? . . . [37] Yet in all these things we are more than conquerors through Him who loved us. [38] For I am persuaded that neither death nor life, nor angels nor principalities nor powers, nor things present nor things to come, [39] nor height nor depth, nor any other created thing, shall be able to separate us from the love of God which is in Christ Jesus our Lord." The love in these verses is made up of Christ's present interceding for us.

God chose us in eternity past with this love. And in this love He planned that we would be conformed to Christ. Then He found us as Gomers — sinful and ungodly — and redeemed us. And then He not only forgave us, on the negative side; but on the positive side, He justified us, He made us right with God. And not only so, He also regenerated us by putting His very life into us. Now, this life within us gives us resurrection power — a power beyond ourselves. Our Lord, as a life-giving Spirit, is resurrection life to us.

God's unconditional love came out of eternity solidly based upon His choice and plan. Then 2,000 years ago, that love was further based in redemption with resurrection and ascension. And now God is loving us from the heavens by interceding for us. His love is present this very moment through His intercession. How marvelous it is when that intercession takes hold of our inner being — when the groanings of the Spirit begin passing through us. Romans 8:26 describes this phenomenon. We find ourselves burdened to pray, not even knowing how to pray for one another, but knowing that the Spirit is interceding with "groanings which cannot be uttered." Yet we are comforted, knowing that Christ "who searches the hearts knows what the mind of the Spirit is, because He makes intercession for the saints according to

God" (Rom. 8:27). The intercession of this One gives us an assurance: "And we know that all things work together for good" (v. 28). The "good" here is the image of God's Son. Thus, the Lord's love flowing through the prayers of the saints is preserving us, keeping us, and making sure that all things are according to God's plan, His eternal purpose — that we would be conformed to the image of His Son (v. 29).

When a believer's living is not according to God's plan, Christ's intercession for them within us will sometimes be with groanings which cannot be uttered. All we can do is say, "O God, we do not know how to pray. Lord, head this one up, head that one up. Do what You need to do. They are rebellious, they are backsliding, they are away from You." We just pray, "God, do it." Then God comes into their environment and causes things to happen. Their life seems to fall apart. There is a sudden turn of events. God hedges up their way with thorns (Hosea 2:6). As they are proceeding in their path that is not according to God's plan but according to their own self-centered life, God makes it difficult for them to continue. The result of God's intervention is that they turn back to the Lord.

So God is loving us in His dealing with us, even in His chastening us: "For whom the LORD loves He chastens, and scourges every son whom He receives" (Heb. 12:6). Our nature is rebellious. We have strayed a thousand times. But His chastening love has been so faithful to bring us back to what He chose us for, to what His plan is, and to why He redeemed us and is living in us. Now He is presently interceding for the saints. What a blessed feeling it is to join in with the Spirit's intercession.

I prayed the other morning, "Lord, this person — his heart
is hard. His heart right now is in that condition; he just cannot
go out to You." But I said, "Lord, it is okay if his heart is hard
because You are the One who said, I will take away the stony
heart out of your flesh." I believe that was Christ's intercession passing through me as I was praying for that person. This
present intercession is the manifestation of God's love toward
His saints. As we are praying, the Lord is interceding in our
prayers. Hallelujah for Christ's faithful intercession in the
prayer life of all the saints (Heb. 7:25). This intercession is
another aspect of the unconditional love of God.

The Spirit's transmission

Finally, let us consider the fifth aspect of God's unconditional love — the Spirit's transmission. Romans 5:5 says,
"The love of God has been poured out in our hearts by the Holy
Spirit who was given to us." The verb "has been poured out"
is in the Greek perfect tense. This tense refers to a present,
continuous state that is based upon something that happened
in the past. This means that the love of God was poured out in
our hearts in the *past* and continues to have a *present* effect
and will continue to have its effect in the *future*.

So whether or not you are conscious of the love of God,
whether or not you have the sensations of that love, it has been
permanently poured out in the region of your heart by the Holy
Spirit. Simply open up your heart and fellowship with the
Lord. Admit that you have lived in your self-life. Confess your
sins. Tell Him everything. Tell Him about the lowest feelings

that you have. Tell Him how stressed out you are. Tell Him. Even bring your feelings of anger to Him. Tell Him, "Lord, I don't understand why this has happened to me." Tell Him. And you will find the love of God poured out in your heart through the Holy Spirit.

God's love is made up of the Spirit's transmission. The Spirit transmits all that is in this love — God's choice and His plan, Christ's redemption, resurrection, ascension, and intercession. Now we can have the reality of this love in our experience. We can be in "the good of it" by the Holy Spirit. Jude 20-21 says, [20] "But you, beloved, building yourselves up on your most holy faith, praying in the Holy Spirit, [21] keep yourselves in the love of God." The participial phrase, "praying in the Holy Spirit," modifies the verb, "*keep* yourselves in the love of God." So the way we keep ourselves in the love of God is by praying in the Holy Spirit. When we pray in the Holy Spirit, we enter the realm of the poured-out love of God. This is how we keep our hearts in the unconditional love of God.

It is so easy for a day to go by — you go to work and come home. Maybe you have been burdened down with all the cares of life and have had no prayer and fellowship with the Lord. You feel somewhat beaten down. And you feel like God does not love or care about you that much. You do not have the present enjoyment of His love in your sensation. But Jude tells us, "Keep yourselves in the love of God." Take some initiative now. Do not go away from the love, but keep yourself in it. He tells you how — "praying in the Holy Spirit." It is not praying just from your mind, but praying in the Holy Spirit. That means you use your spirit to pray, fellowship, talk, call out, cry out, and sing. This activates your spirit and brings you into the realm of the Holy Spirit. Sometimes there is a breaking-through period, but the principle is that we can keep ourselves in the love of God. This is God's unconditional love toward us through the Spirit's transmission.

As we see the composition of God's love we discover that it is not just a shallow, superficial feeling in God. This love is eternal. This love can never be defeated or frustrated, because it met the devil, it met sin, it met every obstacle, and it overcame. It overcame through death, through resurrection, and through ascension. And now this love is transmitted into us by the Holy Spirit.

God's unconditional love — the perfection of the church

The love of God moves us, preserves us, keeps us, and reaches us wherever we are. And this very love is the love we have toward one another in the church. This unconditional love of God is the love with which we love one another. This is what makes the perfect church. The perfect church is the church that has the love of God flowing in all the imperfect members toward all the other imperfect members. All the members, with all their imperfections, are in a fellowship with one another in the love of God.

In Matthew 5:48 when the Lord said, "You shall be perfect, just as your Father in heaven is perfect," He was not speaking of a moral kind of perfection — having a completely righteous and rectified life without any problems, faults, or sins. Of course, we are not condoning sin; but here the Lord was not referring to a sinless life. When we think of "perfect," we think of living a perfect life of absolute holiness according to God's standard. But here the context of being perfect is Matthew 5:44: "But I say to you, love your enemies, bless those who curse you, do good to those who hate you, and pray for those who spitefully use you and persecute you." This means "Love the unlovable." Love the ones who are irritating to you. Love your enemies. Then He says, "Therefore you shall be perfect, just as your Father in heaven is perfect." This means that the Father's love is perfect toward all sinful men. That is the meaning of perfection. Also, in Colossians 3:14 Paul tells the believers, "Put on love, which is the bond of perfection," or "the bond of perfectness." Thus, there can be a perfect church.

What is the perfect church? It is a forgiving church. It is a longsuffering church. It is an enduring, patient, caring church that is receiving all the failing, sinful, ungodly people who have Christ in them. There is forgiveness up to seventy times seven (Matt. 18:22). And there is love and there is mercy. There is this kind of relationship that you do not find in any other place. In our past, when someone treated us unfairly or we were offended, we may have left and gone somewhere else. But that does not accomplish the Lord's desire to perfect the church in the realm of God's unconditional love. This is the meaning of His prayer in John 17:23, "that they may be made perfect into one." Being perfected into one is simply this: the love of God is being perfected in us toward one another. This does not mean the perfecting of your condition. It means the perfecting of my response to your condition —

how I receive you, love you, pray for you, and have mercy toward you. It is how I receive you and make you the object of God's love, no matter what condition you are in.

The church is filled with the love of God — the love He has toward us, the love we have toward Him, and the love we have toward one another. How marvelous that this is the love in the church. The love life in the church is the unconditional love of God coming to us. We know what He has done for us. We know how He has received us. Now that same love is demonstrated toward one another. How important it is to make a phone call to encourage a saint. How important it is to fix some soup for someone who is ill. How important it is to provide a meal when a family is needy. Or when a wife has had the children all week, how important it is for the husband to say, "Honey, I will take care of the kids tonight." How important it is to give our money, rather than being stingy with it. Give it to your wife, give it to your husband, give it to one another. And give it cheerfully. God loves a cheerful giver. How important it is to demonstrate His love even when someone does not deserve it.

Sometimes in our lowest state, we are shocked when God's love comes to us through someone. For example, not long ago, when I was feeling unlovely, someone happened to call on the phone and say, "Brother Bill, the Lord spoke to me yesterday and said, I love Bill Freeman." That really touched me. It infused me. They heard from the Lord that He loves me! Wow!

We love Him because He first loved us. We are human — we all need some demonstration of that love. And if we follow life and follow the Spirit, that love will be manifesting itself in different ways through us. Oh, may the Lord make us distinguishable — "By this all will know" that we are His disciples. The church is a group of people who are simply in love with Jesus and loving one another. Oh, may the Lord manifest this more and more.

7

The Perfection of God's Unconditional Love

Knowing the truth concerning God's love in our relationship with Him has a life-changing effect on us. When Jesus said in John 8:32, "And you shall know the truth, and the truth shall make you free," that included knowing the truth and reality of God's unconditional love. To know this realm does something within us. It frees us. The realm where God's love flows is the realm that makes us free indeed (John 8:36). It is not that we can point to a definite experience that changed us; but within us there is a dawning, a gradual realization that God loves us, not because of our condition, but simply because *He* chose to make us the objects of His love. This sets us free. The more we see the love of God operating in an unconditional way over us, the more we are set free from an abnormal relationship with the Lord.

First John 4:18 says, "There is no fear in love; but perfect love casts out fear, because fear involves torment." Perfect love, which is God's unconditional love, is the love that casts out fear. Negatively, fear can characterize our relationship with the Lord. If we have a fearful relationship with God, it will be insecure and not solid. We will not have boldness in the day of judgment (1 John 4:17); neither will we have boldness at His appearing (1 John 2:28). This is because the relationship we have is characterized by fear based on an erroneous idea of God and His relationship to us. Such a relationship with Him, characterized by great insecurity and feelings of fear, is a tormenting experience.

"Perfect love casts out fear." This means our relationship with the Lord begins to be characterized by the unconditional, perfect love of God toward us. We are secure in that love that we see demonstrated and defined in detail in the book of Hosea. God's love pursued Gomer through every kind of failing condition. When you realize that the unconditional love of God is surrounding you, your relationship will be characterized by perfect love. The more we see the perfect love of God, the more our inward being will calm down and be tranquil. Our relationship with the Lord will be comfortable, without torment and fear. We will rest with great security in His everlasting love. This shows us what a difference the love of God makes in our whole relationship with Him.

We have seen the basic revelation of God's unconditional love, and we have also seen that the nature of that love is related to the Father, the Son, and the Spirit. It is the Father's choice and plan that makes up this love, as well as the Son's redeeming work, resurrection, ascension, and present intercession. Also included in the nature of God's love is the Spirit's transmission of all that God has planned for us and all that God feels toward us. So basically, the nature of God's unconditional love is just God Himself — the Father, the Son, and the Spirit — in His choosing us, redeeming us, and then coming into us as the life-giving Spirit to impart all the riches of His nature for us to enjoy .

After seeing the basic revelation of God's love and its nature, let us consider the perfection of God's unconditional love. This is a crucial matter because it can revolutionize our idea of the church and the way believers are to be related to one another on this earth.

Concepts of "The Perfect Church"

What is the standard of perfection for the church, God's people? To answer this we need to look at the concepts of what the ideal church should be and what the ultimate goal and purpose of the church is. Throughout church history and even today there are many different concepts of the ideal church. Now let us consider a few.

Doctrinal purity

Some believers may have the concept that the ideal for the church is doctrinal purity. They think that if we could just get a group of believers who are doctrinally clear concerning so many aspects of the Christian faith, then this would be the real expression of the Body of Christ. When this point of doctrinal purity is of supreme importance among believers, the main question in their fellowship is, "Where are you doctrinally?" This is particularly true of those groups of Christians who hold a strict dispensational understanding of Scripture. Such understanding includes the seven dispensations, with the pre-tribulation rapture of the church and the pre-millennial coming of the Lord according to a prophetic schedule. These believers are strong to point out the exact difference in the interpretation of Scripture related to Israel and the church. To their understanding, certain verses in the New Testament are strictly for the Jews, while other verses, including Paul's Epistles, are strictly for the church. Thus, you should not apply verses to the Jews which should be applied to the church. When these believers are with other believers, they may focus solely on these fine points of doctrine and measure the others according to their standard of doctrinal purity. Of course, I am not suggesting that we not care for doctrine. But we have to see that the standard of perfection for the church is not that we all agree on these finer points of doctrine.

As believers we all have to know that there is a difference between the essential truths of the faith, which have been "once for all delivered to the saints" (Jude 3), and the many various teachings that believers differ on. There are certain truths that are crucial, that have to do with our salvation. Believing in these truths determines our eternal destiny — that is, we are not lost but saved. These truths are related to (1) the Triune God — the Father, the Son, and the Spirit — eternally and simultaneously coexisting as Three in One; and (2) the Person and work of Christ. He is God and He is man in His one Person; and He died for us on the cross, shedding His blood that we might be redeemed and reconciled to God by faith and not by works. We are saved not by trying to do something to please God from our self, but simply by believing in the finished work of Christ and being regenerated by the Holy Spirit. For these truths Paul said, "I have fought the good fight, I have finished the race, I have kept the faith" (2 Tim. 4:7).

Concerning the truths related to man's salvation, there is no compromise and there is no toleration of any other gospel. Paul emphatically said in Galatians 1:8-9, [8] "But even if we, or an angel from heaven, preach any other gospel to you than what we have preached to you [the gospel of the saving grace of the Lord Jesus], let him be accursed. [9] As we have said before, so now I say again, if anyone preaches any other gospel to you than what you have received, let him be accursed." So the importance of this truth is clear.

As Christians we all hold this common truth of salvation through faith. But there are many differences of belief in other areas, such as baptism. For example, some believers baptize by immersion, while others baptize by sprinkling. And there are also believers who do not practice baptism at all. These are all real born-again people, yet they have some differences in interpretation and understanding of Scripture. There are also differences among believers regarding the details of the Lord's coming. Some believe that the whole church will be raptured before the great tribulation — at any hour, any moment. Yet there are also many Christians who believe that the whole church will pass through the tribulation and be raptured at the end. And still other Christians believe that the whole church will not be raptured together, but that there will be several raptures during the tribulation, from the beginning to the end, according to each believer's readiness.

With all the innumerable differences among believers concerning the details of doctrines, it seems like an impossible task for us to meet together to express God based upon doctrinal purity. Even husbands and wives may not agree with each other on all these points. Nevertheless, among some believers doctrinal purity is an ideal of what the church should be.

Historical continuity

Another ideal is historical continuity, which means that the proper church should be able to trace back its lineage historically, with continuity. This is particularly related to the institutions of the Roman Catholic Church and the Episcopal Church. The focus and the ideal for their existence is historical continuity — the ability to trace the succession of all their bishops back to Peter, whom they believe was the first bishop of Rome and eventually the first pope. So this ideal of historical continuity becomes the basis of forming a gathering of believers.

Uniformity of practice

A third ideal is uniformity of practice. Believers who adhere to this ideal base their belief on the Scriptures related to "one accord." The practical outworking of being in one accord is uniformity of practice. Thus, to have proper churches on this earth, all the churches should be uniform in their practice — every church should have the same hymnal and the same Bible translation and preach the same sermons.

Uniformity of practice is strongly emphasized in some religious groups. For example, I once visited some Hutterites, who meet according to the Anabaptist tradition of the Reformation period. They read the printed messages of Jacob Hutter every Sunday morning. In every Hutterite assembly there is no speaker ministering the Word of God, because they feel that no one could improve on Jacob Hutter's messages. So there is a uniformity among them all. Whatever Hutterite community you visit, you will find that on Sunday morning they turn to a certain page in the volumes of Jacob Hutter's sermons and read that message. This is uniformity of practice.

Many believers feel that the ideal church is one that practices everything identically. However, uniformity of practice can become a replacement for the believers' living touch with Christ their Head. Some of the practices may be scripturally proper and good, but the concept behind them is that the ideal church and its expression should be uniform in practice.

Organizational correctness

We have seen that doctrinal purity, historical continuity, and uniformity of practice are three concepts of what the ideal church should be. A fourth ideal is organizational correctness, that is, being proper organizationally. Basically, among believers who have this concept, there is talk like this: "Do you have the fivefold ministry of the apostle, prophet, evangelist, shepherd, and teacher?" Thus, the goal and the ideal of church practice is to organizationally be related by the fivefold ministry. You know who your apostles are, who your prophets are, who your evangelists are, and so forth. Also included in this organizational correctness should be the New Testament structure of elders and deacons, so that the government of the church would not be pastoral. This prohibits a clergy-laity system, which has developed through church history. The New Testament structure of leadership and administration of a local church does not consist of one man but a plurality — a few brothers as elders, as well as deacons and deaconesses. So the ideal or the goal we should arrive at is something organizational, based upon the proper position of the gifts the Lord has given to the Body.

Charismatic manifestations

Fifth, among believers there is also the concept that the ideal church is made up of charismatic manifestations and the gifts of the Spirit. This means that ideally in every meeting the gifts of the Spirit would be manifested, including some of the more outward gifts such as speaking in tongues with interpretation, healings, discerning of spirits, and casting out of demons. Thus, in this view of the ideal church, the gifts of the Spirit must be manifested and practiced.

There are elements of truth in all five of these ideals that we have mentioned. Concerning *doctrinal purity,* we all know there are doctrinal truths in the Bible. We also know that there is a biblical principle of *historical continuity,* but it must be interpreted properly. Do we interpret it to be a succession of bishops or a continuation of the ministry of Paul, Peter, John and the other apostles in the Word of God? There is also *uniformity of practice* among the churches in the New Testament. For example, Paul can speak for all the churches of God when he says, "We have no such custom" of being contentious (1 Cor. 11:16). You would not find a spirit of contention in any of the churches because among the saints there was a spirit-produced spontaneous uniformity in certain things.

In the same way, there are elements of truth in the *organizational correctness*. In the church you have elders in the Lord and apostles who are commissioned by the Lord. *Apostle* is a Greek word and *missionary* is a Latin word. They both mean "sent one." Surely, there have been ones sent by the Lord throughout church history. For example, Hudson Taylor was an apostle to China and opened up the gospel to that country. There are many such gifts in the Body today. So there is truth in organizational correctness.

Also, in the Bible there are the gifts of the Holy Spirit and the *charismatic manifestations* according to those gifts. Some do speak in tongues. There are healings, and there is casting out of demons. Thus, there is truth and biblical principle in all these concepts of the ideal church. But what happens today is that the ideal thought of the church begins to focus in one of these areas so that the *goal* becomes doctrinal purity, historical continuity, uniformity of practice, organizational correctness, or charismatic manifestations.

Whether spoken or unspoken, these concepts of the church today are in the thought of many Christians. So to them the perfect church would be a church of doctrinal purity, historical continuity, uniformity of practice, organizational correctness, or charismatic manifestations. These are often the ideal concepts of the perfect church.

The Biblical Revelation of "Perfection"

Being related in the realm of God's love

After seeing man's ideal concepts for the church, let us look into the Word to see the standard of perfection that is revealed for God's people to be together as the church. In the New Testament, the perfection of the church is God's unconditional love flowing between the members. Love is relational. It has to do with how we are related to one another — how we forgive one another, how we receive one another, how we treat one another. All of us belong to the same God, with the same Father, the same Christ, and the same Holy Spirit; and we are being related together in the love of God. Love is personal, and it is related to God's nature and person. In our relationships with each other, love is in contrast to all the impersonal ideals we have mentioned. Doctrines are impersonal. Historical continuity is also impersonal. Even the gifts can be impersonal. And the ideals of uniformity of practice and proper organization are both impersonal. They are not relational.

God is love. He loves and forgives His people. He wants to be related to His people, and He wants His people to be related to one another in Himself in love, rather than merely agreeing on doctrines, practices, uniformity, organization, and gifts. However, because these impersonal things have been the focus among so many believers, the history of the church is filled with division upon division. These divisions, occurring with much heartbreak, hatred, and bitterness between Christians, have resulted from emphasizing a doctrine, a practice, an experience, a personality, or some other matter. These things have come between us as believers and divided us. Sincere and well-intentioned, we may have thought that to be absolute for the Lord was to have doctrinal purity or uniformity of practice, or to have the gifts of the Spirit manifested in a certain way. So what has happened? These ideals have upset our relationships with one another. They have become the very factors of division.

The Lord's table is another example of this. The table of the Lord symbolizes the oneness of the Body — one cup, one bread. When we participate in the table, we are not only declaring the Lord's death on the cross, but we are partaking of one bread. This signifies that we are all members one of another. We are one loaf. The Lord made us one Body.

Though the table symbolizes the oneness among believers, the very practice of the table has become, in church history, a factor of division. For example, the Roman Catholics and the Lutherans are divided over transubstantiation and consubstantiation. The Catholic doctrine of transubstantiation means that the elements are changed into the physical body and blood of Christ. Consubstantiation means that the elements are not actually physically changed, but that the Lord is present in and with the sacraments. Then there was the reformer Ulrich Zwingli's belief that the sacraments were only signs, or symbols, of the Lord's body. Thus, the Catholics were divided from Luther, and Luther was divided from Zwingli. Now the Lord's table, which was intended to express oneness among Christians, itself became a factor of division.

As believers we may have been in this realm of doctrinal debate for years and years, not realizing that the perfection of the church is not here. The perfection of the church is in the realm of the love of God between believers. It is relational. It is not about whether you agree with me on every doctrinal point. But it is about how much I can forgive you; it is about how much forbearance there is between you and I who have differences of feeling about things. How much can we live by the life of Christ in our spirit to bear one another in love, to enjoy and minister to one another, and to deprive ourselves of our own rights for the sake of building up one another in love? *How much can we stay in God together?* In eternity we will not be celebrating doctrinal purity, charismatic gifts, or historical continuity. We will all enjoy being together in the love of God and flowing with one another in that realm. In eternity we will be relational; we will be built together and related by the perfect love of God.

According to the Bible, the perfection of God's unconditional love is to be found in the church. The church becomes the container and the embodiment of His love. In John 13:35 the Lord said, "By this all will know that you are My disciples, if you have love for one another." This love toward one another is the love that gathers together, worships together, prays together, forgives together, drops complaints together, is forbearing together. Even if you are right about a spiritual or doctrinal matter, if it interferes with your relationship with another, you do not hold to your rightness.

Paul was spiritually and doctrinally correct concerning how God felt about believers eating meat that was offered to idols. In Romans 14:14 he says, "I know and am convinced by the Lord Jesus that there is nothing unclean of itself; but to him who considers anything to be unclean, to him it is unclean." Paul was convinced by the Lord that "there is nothing unclean of itself." Yet he is saying that because his brother is offended by his eating, even though it is spiritually and doctrinally right, he will not eat meat in the presence of his brother. This is to walk according to love, and to care for God's building of the church. It is caring for the relationship rather than rightness.

Without this kind of love, marriages are destroyed. In our marriage we know that interference in the relationship is often due to us holding on to what we feel is right. That means that our spouse is wrong and we are right. Rightness becomes the factor in your relationship rather than fellowship, forgiveness, and loving one another with the unconditional love of God.

Rightness destroys relationships. It has damaged the church; it has divided the church. No one would divide unless he felt he was right. Yet Paul transcends the realm of everyone's rightness in 1 Corinthians 13:1-3 by saying, [1] "Though I speak with the tongues of men and of angels, but have not love, I have become as sounding brass or a clanging cymbal. [2] And though I have the gift of prophecy, and understand all mysteries and all knowledge, and though I have all faith, so that I could remove mountains, but have not love, I am nothing. [3] And though I bestow all my goods to feed the poor, and though I give my body to be burned, but have not love, it profits me nothing." In other words, if I am doing everything right, but have not love, I am nothing. My rightness counts as nothing.

So the premium is placed on love rather than on all these other things. It is into this realm of love that God wants to perfect all of us.

Being perfect is loving perfectly

Now let us look further at the Word of God to see the biblical standard for the ideal church. In Matthew 5:43-48 the Lord says, [43] "You have heard that it was said, You shall love your neighbor and hate your enemy. [44] But I say to you, love your enemies, bless those who curse you, do good to those who hate you, and pray for those who spitefully use you and persecute you, [45] that you may be sons of your Father in heaven; for He makes His sun rise on the evil and on the good, and sends rain on the just and on the unjust. [46] For if you love those who love you, what reward have you? Do not even the tax collectors do the same? [47] And if you greet your brethren only, what do you do more than others? Do not even the tax collectors do so? [48] Therefore you shall be perfect, just as your Father in heaven is perfect."

What does it mean to be perfect? It simply means to love perfectly, to have perfect love. Of course, none of us have this love. You do not have it, and I do not have it. This love is of God. It is absolutely intrinsic to His life. To have this love, you have to have His life, because this love is the nature of His life. So the only way to be perfect — to love as God loves — is to have God. The Lord's words in verse 45, "that you may be sons of your Father," prove that perfect love is not something we can generate or work up. It is not a matter of reading

enough about it, studying it enough, or getting enough train-
ing in how to love so that we can do it. That will not work! To
be "sons of your Father" means that you must have the life of
your Father. You need to be begotten with the divine life.
When that life enters us, it comes as a gift — "the gift of God
is eternal life in Christ Jesus our Lord" (Rom. 6:23). We have
to realize that when we receive the life of the Lord Jesus, in
that life is this perfect love that loves the unlovely, the sinners,
the enemies, and that pursues the Gomers and can stand when
everything else has fallen. That love is part of His life. First
John 3:14 says, "We know that we have passed from death to
life, because we love the brethren." We know by the way we
feel about the brothers. There is a feeling of love in us toward
them because we have God's life.

When we fellowship about this kind of love you might
think, "There is no way that I could love like that. If you only
knew how bad I am — how much I have bitterness and hatred
in me." We are all the same and we are all on the same level.
None of us have this love. But now, we have received God's
life; and with that life comes His love. So as we enjoy that life
and drink that life, spontaneously that love will become more
and more a part of our reactions. We will have a disposition
that just reacts with God's love toward any kind of situation.
This is why we need a lot of life, and a lot of enjoyment and
experience of life, allowing that life to flow.

When you take care of anything related to life in you — if
life is not spending that money, if life is not going to that place,
if life is apologizing — if life in you is doing something and
you follow that life, every step of your obedience of life *is* your

loving of the brothers. Our daily personal life is related to me
loving you and you loving me in this way. For example, the
other day I was enjoying the Lord by following Him in my
little habits around the kitchen. I realized that by following the
Lord, I was loving the brothers in a practical way in those
moments. I was getting a disposition of love wrought into me
as a result of taking care of that life.

In 1 John 3:14 we saw that love toward the brothers is the
standard of perfection. Perfection is loving perfectly with
God's unconditional love. Again, this means it is relational. In
other words, instead of looking for doctrinal purity, I am
looking for how I can enjoy Christ with you and be related to
you when we differ doctrinally. This is "to the glory of God"
(Rom. 15:7). This is what is perfect. You do not receive me on
the condition that I will one day see things as you see them and
come to agreement with you. If our relationship is based on
this, there will be another day when we will not agree on still
finer points, and we will be divided by that. This is what has
happened throughout church history. People were so happy
coming together initially. But today, they are all scattered.
Why? Because the focus was not love. Love is relational. It is
God, and He is a person. He loves people. He is not loving
pieces of paper, books, and things like that. He is loving us!

The bond of perfection is love

Let us look at this love in another passage. Colossians 3:14
says, "But above all these things put on love, which is the bond
of perfection." Some versions translate the last part of this

verse as "the bond of perfectness." In Greek, this construction is what is called the genitive of apposition. Literally translated, it means "the bond in which perfection consists." So this love is equal to the bond of perfection. In the divine thought, the love is the perfection. Here in this verse, Paul defines the perfection or perfectness that we are to arrive at as simply *love*.

In the preceding verses of Colossians 3 we see how this love operates. Verse 11 gives us the background: "Where there is neither Greek nor Jew, circumcised nor uncircumcised, barbarian, Scythian, slave nor free, but Christ is all and in all." In the church in Colosse, there were Greeks with their culture and there were Jews with their religion. Some believers were circumcised, and others were not. In the ancient world there were intense feelings about the matter of circumcision and uncircumcision. The Jews called the Gentiles "the uncircumcised" in a very derogatory sense. So in the meetings of the church at Colosse there were people with a Jewish background, who believed strongly in circumcision, and there were also the uncircumcised, the Gentiles. In addition, there were barbarians and Scythians. The latter refers to a very low class of people. Unlike the well-learned, wise Greeks, the Scythians were uneducated. They were sometimes described as savage and uncivilized.

Imagine — there is a refined Jew who knows how to delicately handle everything, eating the proper foods in the proper way. And in the same church there is a crude Scythian. So there are people of widely different cultures, different religious backgrounds, and also different nationalities. And then verse 11 continues, "slaves, free man." This represents social distinctions. At the time Paul wrote to the Colossians there was a slave system. There were masters and there were slaves. That system was there at the time Paul wrote to the Colossians. Thus, in the church there were brothers and sisters, all loving the Lord, enjoying the same Christ, all having equal status as believers. But in society, some of these brothers and sisters were related to one another as masters and slaves. One owned another, telling him what to do every hour of the day because he belonged to him. The purchased slave did not have any rights of his own. On the other hand, he was now a brother in the church. So there were strained relationships among the saints meeting together there in Colosse, due to these conflicting circumstances. But Paul says that in the new man there cannot be cultural, religious, and social distinctions, "but Christ is all and in all." Now, we may say that Christ is all, and even put up a banner declaring "Christ is all and in all." But if you have a background of refined culture and I have a background of barbarianism, when we come together we are going to have some reactions toward each other. This is just part of the natural man, the old man.

Now consider, what would the ideal be if we found ourselves in Colosse with this conglomeration, this melting pot, of people? You might think that the ideal would be to start a Greek church and gather all the Greek believers together. Then we would have our Greek things in common. And someone else could start a Scythian church — the First Church of the Scythians. It would not matter how you came because you would not have to worry about those cultured

Greeks. But Paul does not condone building up churches based upon culture or any other kind of distinction. Those would be further examples of *man's* ideal concept of the church. But Paul says that none of these things exist in the new man, where Christ is all and in all.

Then Paul continues in Colossians 3:12-14, [12] "Therefore, as the elect of God, holy and beloved, put on tender mercies, kindness, humbleness of mind, meekness, longsuffering; [13] bearing with one another, and forgiving one another, if anyone has a complaint against another; even as Christ forgave you, so you also must do. [14] But above all these things put on love, which is the bond of perfection," or "the bond of perfectness." So the expression of this love operates through all of these virtues: the tender mercies, the kindness, the humility, the longsuffering, the forgiving of one another. These are all words expressing Christ with His life and nature. Here we see what perfection is.

The meaning of "every man perfect in Christ"

In Colossians 1:28 Paul speaks more about this perfection: "Him we preach, warning every man and teaching every man in all wisdom, that we may present every man *perfect* in Christ Jesus." Some Bible versions translate "perfect" as "full grown." The Greek word basically refers to reaching the peak of maturity. What does it mean to "present every man perfect in Christ"? Paul explains in the next three verses: [29] "To this end I also labor, striving according to His working which works in me mightily. [2:1] For I want you to know what a great conflict

I have for you and those in Laodicea, and for as many as have
not seen my face in the flesh, ² that their hearts may be
comforted, being knit together in love, and attaining unto all
riches of the full assurance of understanding, unto the full
knowledge of the mystery of God, Christ."

Knowing the background of these verses would help us to
appreciate what Paul is saying here. Many damaging things
had come into the church in Colosse — philosophy, religious
rituals, men's traditions, asceticism. The influence of these
things hurt the saints. Specifically, it hurt their love for one
another because it hurt their hearts. Their relationships with
one another were damaged severely due to so many different
teachings. Some among them were saying, "Do not touch, do
not taste, do not handle," in relation to eating and drinking.
Dogmas like these were being formed, and as a result the
saints were judging each other according to these standards.
The focus was not "Christ in you" but whether or not you were
conforming to the dogmas. This destroyed their love relationship with one another.

Paul came into the Colossian situation with the earnest
desire to "present every man perfect in Christ." Then he shows
us how this will happen: "that their hearts may be...knit
together in love." This is a window into the way we will be
presented perfectly at the judgment seat of Christ. It will not
be according to our standard, but according to how much we
have released the love of God out of our spirit and soul into the
brothers and sisters, so that our hearts are knit together in love.

To be perfect in Christ does not mean to agree perfectly, but
to love perfectly. And to love perfectly means to forgive

perfectly — to be a perfect complaint dropper. Can you drop your complaint? Paul is not in the realm of whether or not your complaint is justified. Your complaint might be justified. You might be right. But he does not care whether you are right or wrong. He simply says that you need to drop your complaint.

I have fellowshipped with brothers and sisters and couples who have had complaints. I have watched the husband and wife oppose each other like they were in a boxing match. The complaint is always over some matter that the husband feels he is right about, while the wife is feeling she is right. And each feels misunderstood by the other. They are both defending their rightness and stirring up yet more disagreement. It seems like they are just throwing dust in the air. But Paul says that if you have a complaint, and you are even legitimately justified in having that complaint, the important thing is not to get your complaint resolved, but to drop it for the sake of the organic relationship, peace, oneness of heart, and forgiveness.

Colossians 3:14 says, "Put on love, which is the bond of perfectness." The perfectness is us being related together in the love of God. Seeing this makes all the difference in how we view the church, how the church meets, and what the goal of the church is. If our goal is anything less than God Himself, who is love, we are missing the perfection. We are missing it even if we have the greater gifts of prophecy, all knowledge, and all faith (1 Cor. 13:2). The perfection of the church is simply in loving all the failing Gomers with God's love. Christ loved the church. Though the church was a failure, alienated from Him and ungodly, He gave Himself for her because she was the object of His love.

This is God's love. We do not have this love naturally, but it is in us as a gift. It has been poured out in our hearts. And when we keep ourselves in the love of God by praying in the Holy Spirit, we are actually in a place of oneness with all believers everywhere. We are in the realm of the love of God. Between us all is this standard of perfection.

Being brought into a state of perfection

John 17:23 is a very crucial passage among us today as believers because we all desire the oneness it reveals. In this verse the Lord says, "I in them, and You in Me." When He says, "You in Me," He is referring to the Father in Him. The Father loves Him and He is "into the bosom of the Father" (John 1:18). This speaks of the mutual love between the Father and the Son. The first part of John 17:23 says, "I in them," which means the Son is in us. Of course, when the Son is in us, that means the Father is in us, because the Son comes with the Father. He comes with their love relationship. He comes with this wonderful liquid love flowing between the Father and the Son, and the Son and the Father. He is in us moving with that love. In John 15:9 He says, "As the Father loved Me, I also have loved you; abide in My love." Let that love move in you. That means let the divine life flow. When the life flows, the love flows. When you release life, love comes with that life.

"I in them" means "I am moving in them, I am loving in them." It is a love relationship. The Lord wants to establish in us a relationship with Him and the Father that casts out all fear.

He wants us to be comfortable with Him. He wants us to know the security of His love. As the Father has loved the Son, the Son loves us. He wants us to know that love. He wants our whole relationship to be in that love. He wants us to know that even when we are failing, we are loved by Him. He died for us. He wants us to know the security of coming to Him after a horrible defeat and saying, "Jesus, forgive me." He wants us to know, in the security of that love, that the blood is cleansing us from all sin.

The first part of John 17:23 says, "I in them, and You in Me." The next word is "that," which can also be translated "in order that." In Greek it is the word ἵνα, which introduces a purpose clause. Thus, "I in them, and You in Me" is for a purpose — "that they may be made perfect into one." This can also be rendered "that they may be perfected into one." The verb "perfected" is in the perfect tense, indicating a present state or reality based on a past action. So the thought here is simply this: "in order that they may be in a state of perfection," which means "in order that they may be in a state of unconditional love." Then we have the words "into one," showing us that the real oneness of believers today can only be arrived at when together we are in a state of God's unconditional love.

Verse 23 continues with another purpose clause: "In order that the world may know that You have sent Me, and have loved them as You have loved Me." It is based on this highest prayer that believers today appeal to the Body of Christ to be one. The Lord prayed that we all would be perfected into one, but we have to look carefully at this verse to see how this is realized. Because we are loved unconditionally, our relationship with Him and His relationship with us is altogether in this uninterrupted love state. We are in a love state, in a love fellowship, in a love relationship. We are with Him in this love.

If I myself do not have a love relationship with the Lord in this kind of way, it will be difficult for me to relate this love to you when you are a Gomer to me. If you are a Gomer, I will leave you because my love is limited. My love can only go so far, and then my relationship with you is finished and I am out the door. This is what happens in marriages. Your love may last for ten years, fifteen years, or maybe even twenty years. But then one day, because it is your love, something will happen to cause it to run out. This just shows that we need another love, which means we need another life.

This brings us back to the Lord's words in John 17:23, "I in them." He is in us as Another life with another love in order that we may be perfected, or be in a state of perfection. This simply means to be in a state of the unconditional love of God flowing out of us and into others, making us one. The real oneness is the perfect love between us, and it does not require uniformity of practice, organizational perfection, and other various ideals set forth by men throughout church history. It requires the love of God and the heart of God to forgive, to receive one another, and to enjoy and stay in that liquid love together.

Let us all ask the Lord to make clear to us that the standard of perfection for the church is this perfect love. This kind of perfection is what the Lord desires on the earth. The standard and highest experience we can have together as believers is enjoying the love of God with one another vertically and horizontally. The Lord tells us that by this love all men will know that we are His disciples. This love is also the atmosphere in which the building of the church takes place. It is the building up in love that Ephesians 4:16 talks about.

In Ephesians 4:13 Paul describes believers as being in a process of arriving at a goal: "Till we all arrive at the oneness of the faith and of the full knowledge of the Son of God, to a perfect man, to the measure of the stature of the fullness of Christ." We may have the thought that the "perfect man" means that we all would be practicing the church life in a certain way. But it actually means that we are all going to be loving in a certain way. The perfect man is a man that embodies the perfect, unconditional love of God toward one another. If you are looking for a perfect church in any other realm, you are looking for things — for practices, for doctrines, for gifts. And eventually you will be disappointed, and in your disappointment you will go from one place to another. But if we are renewed by the Word of God, we will see that the standard of perfection is love — God's love. And out of His love and forgiveness, we grow together in the Lord. Then the Lord will have a way on this earth with all of us. As His people we will be an expression of the love of God.

8

Relationships in God's Unconditional Love

God's standard of perfection

We probably all have our own idea of what *perfect* is — of what *ideal* is. This ideal of perfection can also be applied to our concept and thought about the church. No doubt, we all have had our thought about what the ideal church is. But the revelation of God's standard of perfection and His thought about what is an ideal church can be reduced to ideal relationships.

What is an ideal relationship? What are its components? What are its standards? What would you expect in an ideal relationship? We have our thought about what makes a situation ideal, both in our relationship to the church and our relationships with one another day by day — in marriage life, in family life, on the job. But when we open to the Lord's revelation in His Word, we see God's thought of what is ideal or perfect. God's standard of perfection is His perfect love. This is the ideal — God's love.

Let us look again at what the Lord says in Matthew 5:44-45: [44] "But I say to you, love your enemies, bless those who curse you, do good to those who hate you, and pray for those who spitefully use you and persecute you, [45] that you may be sons of your Father in heaven." The Lord implies here that this kind of love toward our enemies is related to the divine life within us. "That you may be sons of your Father" does not mean that we are just outwardly imitating Him. Rather, it means that we have the Father's life, and we are loving out of that life. The kind of love that is in the Father's life is this love that can love its enemies.

Then the Lord concludes His thought in verse 48: "Therefore you shall be perfect, just as your Father in heaven is perfect." The context requires that we understand this perfection to be a perfecting in loving. And this perfect kind of love is God's love toward His enemies — toward sinners, toward the ungodly. This is God's love. And as His sons, we also are to be perfect in our love toward our enemies. So the perfection has to do with perfect love, and this perfect love has to do with our relationships.

Ideal concepts of the church

We have seen that among believers throughout church history, there have been many ideal concepts of the church. Some have understood the ideal church to be a church that has (1) doctrinal purity or (2) historical continuity or (3) uniformity of practice or (4) organizational correctness or (5) charismatic manifestations. There are all kinds of concepts and practices today among believers. And the thought behind each concept is, "If everyone would just do this, we would have an ideal church." For example, some would say, "If everyone would just adhere to our doctrines, we would have an ideal church of doctrinal purity."

Impersonal things versus relationships in God's love

Let us come to the Word of God to understand what is ideal. All these ideals we have just mentioned are impersonal, not relational. They are not focused on relationships together in the love of God, but they are focused on outward agreement concerning a certain practice, a certain leader, a certain idea, a certain thought, or a certain organization. These things are versus the ideal of love toward one another. They are versus the perfection of our relationships in the love of God.

In the Word the focus is not on something impersonal, but on God Himself between us, on our relationships with one another in God's life with God's love. This is the New Testament standard of perfection — relationships in love, in mercy, and in compassion. The focus is upon being together as believers in the love of God, even though we may have differences of practice, or even though we may like and be helped by certain brothers' ministries more than others'. These differences and preferences may exist, but they are not the focus. The focus is always the love, mercy, and compassion of God.

Keep in mind the phrase in Matthew 5:48 that concludes with, "Therefore you shall be perfect, just as your Father in heaven is perfect." Then read Luke's version of this passage: 35 "But love your enemies, do good, and lend, hoping for nothing in return; and your reward will be great, and you will be sons of the Highest. For He is kind to the unthankful and evil. [36] Therefore be merciful [or, compassionate], just as your Father also is merciful" (Luke 6:35-36). Matthew says, "You shall be perfect, just as your Father in heaven is perfect." But Luke says, "Be merciful, just as your Father also is merciful." So Luke explains Matthew by defining what perfection is. Of course, Matthew defines perfection in the context of God's love. Together these two passages show us that perfection is bringing the love of God into our relationships.

What do we bring into our relationships?

Luke unmistakably defines the real meaning of perfection. Perfection is bringing the love of God into our relationships. What do we bring into our relationships? Do we bring an ideal thought? Or do we bring the love of God? What do we bring into our relationships with one another in the church? What do we bring into our relationship in our marriage? What attitude do we come with? What is our standard? Is it an ideal concept that we all have to conform to or measure up to? What we bring into our relationships determines the reality we have between us. The divine standard of perfection is to bring the love of God into our relationships. What we bring is God's kind of love.

If in the church life we bring God's love into our relationships, "that which is perfect has come" (1 Cor. 13:10). When that which is perfect has come, then everything else is clearly on a much lower level. Paul says it well in 1 Corinthians 13:11: "When I was a child, I spoke as a child, I understood as a child, I thought as a child; but when I became a man, I put away childish things." According to the context of this verse we could paraphrase Paul in this way: "When I was immature in my Christian life, I related to other Christians on the basis of prophecy, speaking in tongues, having great faith, giving my body to be burned, and giving my goods to the poor. I was related in things, in practices — even in spiritual things and in good practices. But when I grew up, I began to be related to believers in the love of God." This is God's building. This is what is eternal. Tongues will cease, prophecies will fail, and even knowledge will vanish away; but love will abide forever. This means that God's nature, His essence, embodied in us and between us is His building and His habitation for eternity.

We have the beginning of God's building and the foretaste of it now in this present age in the church life, in our marriage life, in our daily life. When we experience the love of God between us, our focus is not something impersonal, but personal and relational. It is God's kind of love — Calvary love. It is the Father giving the Son on the cross to shed His blood for ungodly sinners who do not deserve a thing. God's love toward the world is demonstrated in this way.

Love is relational

Knowing that God's love is personal and relational, we can better understand what Paul is saying in 1 Corinthians 13. Let us read verses 1-3: [1] "Though I speak with the tongues of men and of angels, but have not love, I have become as sounding brass or a clanging cymbal. [2] And though I have the gift of prophecy, and understand all mysteries and all knowledge, and though I have all faith, so that I could remove mountains, but have not love, I am nothing. [3] And though I bestow all my goods to feed the poor, and though I give my body to be burned, but have not love, it profits me nothing." All these things are what we usually consider the ideal: a faith church, a mountain-removing church, or a giving-to-the-poor church. Of course, all these things are in the life of God, and God does do these things. But we must ask, What is the focus? What is the emphasis? What is the holding factor between us as believers? What keeps us together? What maintains us together in God's building on this earth?

In 1 Corinthians 13:4-7, as Paul defines love, you realize it is altogether relational, that is, it is in relationship with others in the Body: [4] "Love suffers long and is kind; love does not envy; love does not parade itself, is not puffed up; [5] does not behave rudely, does not seek its own, is not provoked, thinks no evil; [6] does not rejoice in iniquity, but rejoices in the truth; [7] bears all things, believes all things, hopes all things, endures all things." These verses describe relationships. Specifically, they describe relationships with fallen people — people who make mistakes, people who sin, people who are just as they are. The divine love relates in this way to others as well as to ourselves.

Paul continues to elevate love far above all else in verses 8-10: [8] "Love never fails. But whether there are prophecies, they will fail; whether there are tongues, they will cease; whether there is knowledge, it will vanish away. [9] For we know in part and we prophesy in part. [10] But when that which is perfect has come, then that which is in part will be done away."

All these verses from chapter 13 show us that "that which is perfect" is the love of God. However, some interpret "that which is perfect" to be the Scriptures. They reason that because the Scriptures have come, there is no need for speaking in tongues today. But the context does not indicate that the Scriptures are what is being referred to in verse 10. The context here and the broader context of the whole New Testament requires us to understand that what is perfect is the divine love. This love *comes* both now among believers and in a higher, greater, and ultimate sense with the Lord's coming back and for eternity. So we can see that the focus of our relationships is love.

Love issuing out of life

Knowing that God's unconditional love is the perfection, we need to see how this love is the factor in our relationships with one another, and how we can experience relationships in God's unconditional love. First, we have to see the source of this love in our relationships. In John 17:23 the Lord says, "I in them, and You in Me; that they may be made perfect into one, and that the world may know that You have sent Me, and have loved them as You have loved Me."

Again, the words "made perfect" are in the perfect tense. Also, they are in the passive voice, indicating that something is happening to the subject in the sentence. (The active voice means that the subject is acting, and the passive voice means that the subject is being acted upon.) The perfect tense indicates that the effect of what happened in the past continues to be a present state and reality. When the Lord prayed, "that they may be *made perfect*," He used the perfect tense of the Greek verb. This tells us that He was not referring to a *process* of being perfected. He was identifying a *state* of perfection that we are in. Kenneth S. Wuest, in his *Expanded Translation* of the New Testament, translates verse 23 in a way that expresses the significance of the perfect tense: "I in them and you in me, in order that they, having been brought to the state of perfection with respect to oneness, may persist in that state of perfection." In other words, being brought to a state of perfection is simply equal to Christ indwelling us with the Father.

The "I in them" is inseparably linked to the "You in Me." "I in them" means that the Son is in us. "You in Me" means that the Father is in the Son. So we have the Father in the Son as the Spirit flowing into us as our state of perfection. This perfection is the perfection of the oneness existing between the Father and the Son. That oneness comes into us when Christ comes into us. Therefore, perfection is not what we *attain;* it is what we *obtain* when we receive Christ. In every relationship in the Body of Christ, recognize the existing perfection, and then persist and continue in it.

"I in them, and You in Me" denotes an organic union of ourselves with the Triune God in life. Now the purpose of this life is "that they may be made perfect into one." The original Greek language is more specific and is literally translated, "I in them, and You in Me, in order that they might be in a state of perfection." This state, or condition, of perfection is a state of enjoying the love of God. This same perfect passive verb, *made perfect,* is used four times in 1 John in the identical grammatical construction. Each time it refers to a state of being perfected in His love: "in order that you might be in a state of perfection," which is the state of enjoying the unconditional love of God — enjoying His love, His forgiveness, His mercy.

This relationship with Christ, who loves us, is characterized by love, and not fear and torment. I am in a state of perfection in my relationship with the Lord when I am a person who can enjoy the love of God through every kind of situation. When I am enjoying His love toward me in my unworthiness, that love is just flowing out of me toward others. So there is both a vertical and a horizontal relationship of love. That is what constitutes this state of perfection.

Because we have God's life in us, we can be in the enjoyment of God's love. When John 17:23 says, "That they may be made perfect *into one,*" it means that there is an expression. Eventually the world will begin to see and to believe. Because the believers are enjoying life, they are in a state of love. And because they are in a state of love, there is an expression of oneness. And because there is an expression of oneness, the world believes.

This oneness is not a oneness of uniformity, a oneness around an organizational thought, or a oneness of certain practices. It is a oneness that is characterized by a relationship with one another that cannot be broken. It is a oneness out from the unconditional love of God, with forgiveness and mercy and all that is included in that love. All of this is in the divine life. We do not have this kind of love in ourselves. No

one has it! It is gift-love! It is love you receive. It is love that
flows into you. It is love that is part of the nature of God
Himself, who is life. The nature of His life is to love. Just as
every kind of life has a life-necessity, it is a necessity of God's
life to love. He cannot but love.

Let me illustrate this principle of life-necessity. We have a
little cat. It has a cat's life. And the necessity of a cat's life is
to imagine things and then dart around the house in a playful
way. The necessity of her life is to act that way. Who taught
the cat to do that? No one. It is part of the cat life. In the same
way, the necessity of the human life is to feel and to think,
because emotions and thought are part of human life. If you
have human life, you are under the necessity to think and to
feel and to choose. It is part of the nature of human life. Also,
with the divine life there is a necessity, and that necessity is to
love. God is love. He cannot go against His nature. His nature
is to love unconditionally — to love sinners, to reconcile them
to Himself, and then to continue to nourish and cherish them
in their sinful state, in their weakness, in their trials, in their
failures. This is Christ who loved the church and gave Himself
for her, and then continues to nourish and cherish her. So the
necessity of God's life toward the church is to love. In the
same sense, when we genuinely enjoy the divine life and
experience it, we find that the necessity of that life in our being
is to love one another.

First John 4:7 says, "Beloved, let us love one another, for
love is out of God; and everyone who loves is born of God and
knows God." In the first part of this verse, John is telling us to
love one another with the love that is out of God. It is not our

human love that we love with. In the last part of the verse, John brings us to the source of the love: "everyone who loves is born of God and knows God." This means that if we are not begotten of God — regenerated with the life of God in our spirit — there cannot be this quality and kind of God-love.

The source of this love is the divine life. It is the life that has been imparted into us through regeneration. The day we receive Christ, that life comes into our spirit. And it is *in* that life and *with* that life that we love. We bring this kind of love into our relationships. So our love is not a facade. It is not an outward, artificial behavior. It is not trying to put on a Christian demeanor, and love like Christians should love. It is not that we in ourselves are trying to be loving. But the love comes from the life of God. It is altogether the issue of His life. Thus, when we are talking about God's unconditional love and loving one another in this realm, it is not a matter of deciding that we will all love one another in our own natural way. We have to realize that the source of this love is ever the divine life.

Fellowship and obedience activate love

There are two things that will activate God's love in our being and cause it to flow out spontaneously. The first is our fellowship with the Lord. This has to do with the degree of our own enjoyment of the divine life. If we are a person partaking of the divine nature, fellowshipping with the Lord, and drawing from the riches of His grace, then that life of love will manifest itself.

The second thing that will activate God's love in us is obedience. Fellowship and obedience are the two sure ways to experience the love of God and to love with that kind of love. If I am short of fellowship and if I am short of obedience to the Lord, then no matter how much knowledge I may have about loving, I am not going to find that much love on the surface of my being. I will not find it in my inward parts because I am not activating it that much. So I am left to my own efforts, which eventually run out. But the more I live fellowshipping with the Lord and obeying Him all day long — the more I follow the life that comes out of the fellowship of life and obey it and stay with it — the more love will be the issue. This is the revelation in the Word of God.

To see this, let us look at 1 John 2:5: "But whoever keeps His word, truly the love of God is perfected in him. By this we know that we are in Him." This verse shows us that by our obedience the love of God is perfected in our being. This means its reality comes forth. Then John 15:9 says, "As the Father loved Me, I also have loved you; abide in My love." You may say, "Tell me, Lord, how do I abide? I want to abide now. This sounds so good, so wonderful." He tells us in verse 10, "If you keep My commandments, you will abide in My love, just as I have kept My Father's commandments and abide in His love."

These are the same commandments that John speaks of in 1 John 5:3: "For this is the love of God, that we keep His commandments. And His commandments are not burden-some." And immediately after he says that God's command-ments are not burdensome or grievous, he adds, "For whatever is born of God overcomes the world" (v. 4). John quickly turns us to the life of God within us because he knows that whatever these commandments are, they are related to the supply of that life within our being. These life-commandments are the instant speakings that we have during the day, for example, "Do not look at that," or "Do not say it in that way." This is not burdensome; it is coming out of the fellowship of life. Because I am in the fellowship of this life, I experience the sensitivity of its nature. I experience the necessity of its nature, which is to love the Father and to follow Him, "to refuse the evil and choose the good" (Isa. 7:15).

The necessity of that life in me is to follow the Lord in my daily living. When I follow Him as life, I am following His commandments, and they are not burdensome. It is not as if I am down here and God is up in heaven telling me what to do, and then I am trying to do it. It is not like that. God is imparting Himself as life and supply into us, giving us an installation of divine power with everything that pertains to "life and godliness" (2 Pet. 1:3). Then He tells us to take a step, to walk with Him. He has already installed His life into us, but there is still a step needed, a step of obedience. When we take that step of obedience, there is a deeper perfecting of the love of God in our relationships with one another. As we live in fellowship and obedience, we will be able, with an ability given to us by God Himself, to bring God's unconditional love into our relationships.

But if we live disobedient — if you and I are not walking in the light that we already know God wants us to walk in, if we are holding back, if there is hidden sin that has not been repented of and forsaken, if there is some worldly thing that the divine life requires us to let go of, and we are not obeying the speaking within us — we cannot bring God's unconditional love into our relationships. Instead, we will be left holding a grudge, misreading things, getting offended, stumbling, not being able to relate, being hurt, blaming, being bitter, feeling sorry for ourself. We will not be able to find within our being the love of God.

Rather than trying to work up the love, just be a person who loves the Lord and stays in fellowship with Him. Simply "trust and obey," as the words of the hymn declare, "for there's no other way to be happy in Jesus, but to trust and obey." By living an obedient life and keeping His commandments, I abide in His love. And this is how I bring that love into all my relationships in the church. So the source of God's love is His life, and His life lived out in us is the way to love.

We can see this same principle in Colossians 3. Paul says in verse 4, "Christ who is our life." Then notice the progression. Because Christ is our life, Paul says in verses 5-6, [5] "Therefore put to death your members which are on the earth: fornication, uncleanness, passion, evil desire, and covetousness, which is idolatry. [6] Because of these things the wrath of God is coming upon the sons of disobedience." This means that out of the source of the divine life, out of Christ being our life, we can put to death all these evil things related to the moral realm, the sexual realm. And if there was ever a time and ever a generation that needs to hear this kind of word, it is now. Our culture is filled with these immoral things.

The first few verses of Colossians 3 reveal that a person in the fellowship of life seeks "those things which are above." Then out of that fellowship comes obedience in the areas mentioned in verse 5. And then the obedience becomes finer. In verses 7-9 Paul says, [7] "in which you also once walked when you lived in them. [8] But now you must also put off all these: anger, wrath, malice, blasphemy, filthy language out of your mouth. [9] Do not lie to one another...." In other words, widen the scope of your obedience. First, you obey in the matters mentioned in the beginning verses. Then as the divine life is growing, more obedience is required. Paul says in verses 12-13, [12] "Therefore, as the elect of God, holy and beloved, put on tender mercies, kindness, humbleness of mind, meekness, longsuffering; [13] bearing with one another, and forgiving one another, if anyone has a complaint against another; even as Christ forgave you, so you also must do." Then we come to verse 14: "But above all these things put on love, which is the bond of perfection."

So the fellowship of life in the first few verses is followed by a string of obediences in specific areas, from putting to death immoral practices to not lying to one another. This issues in a heart of compassion, kindness, forgiveness, and the love of God that is necessary for the church life. We can see again that the source of love is life and that the life in us requires fellowship and obedience. These two things, fellowship and obedience, will cause love to spring forth; and then we can bring God's love into our relationships.

The atmosphere of love

Finally, as we enjoy the source of life for the love to grow, there will be the reality of love in our relationships. This love produces between us a kind of atmosphere that is without fear. This atmosphere is described in 1 John 4:18: "Perfect love casts out fear." Thus, when the love of God is perfected in us by fellowship and obedience, there is an atmosphere that characterizes our relationships. Because perfect love casts out fear, our relationships are not characterized by fear.

In some church groups the predominant atmosphere that rules is fear: fear if you do not conform to a practice, fear if you are a certain way. There is fear in the relationships because everything is so impersonal. God's unconditional love is not there, so the atmosphere is one of fear. But perfect love casts out fear; and this perfect love is the divine love being perfected in us by our enjoyment of life and following life. Then our relationships are characterized as being without tormenting fear.

First John 4:16-19 says, [16] "And we have known and believed the love that God has for us. God is love, and he who abides in love abides in God, and God in him. [17] Love has been perfected among us in this: that we may have boldness in the day of judgment; because as He is, so are we in this world. [18] There is no fear in love; but perfect love casts out fear, because fear involves torment. But he who fears has not been made perfect in love. [19] We love Him because He first loved us." In these verses, which are very deep, John is describing the nature of perfect love. This kind of love not only casts out fear, but it also gives us boldness in the day of judgment.

There is a reason for our having boldness: "because as He is, so are we in this world." It does not say "as He was" but "as He is." How is He? The Lord Jesus has once and for all passed through Calvary, the tomb, and the grave. His relationship with the Father can never again be characterized by judgment as the One "smitten by God" on the cross (Isa. 53:4). His present relationship with the Father in resurrection is characterized by the eternal flow of love between them. Just *as He is* enjoying this realm of love with the Father, *so are we* in this world. Thus, what characterizes my relationship with God is not judgment, condemnation, or fear, but a sweet rest in the security of that love over me *in this world* — in my condition — because God loves me just as I am. We are enjoying Him and we are with Him, just as the Son is.

Our relationship with the Lord is characterized by love-dealings. All our dealings with the Lord are actually love-dealings. Everything is love. The Lord's discipline in our lives is a love-dealing; it is altogether characterized by love. We love Him because He first loved us and rid the atmosphere between us of any torment and fear.

Brothers and sisters, in your marriage life what kind of attitude and atmosphere do you bring into your relationship? Is your relationship with your spouse characterized by fear? Fear has torment. And when a relationship is characterized by fear and torment, it indicates that there is a kind of demand or expectancy involved. Something other than God's perfect love is the factor determining the relationship. Many times there are ordinances and standards and thoughts. In Ephesians

2:15, on the cross the Lord destroyed the ordinances as well as the enmity, or bad feelings, and the fear that ordinances produce.

The Greek word for *ordinance* is *dogma* (δόγμα), which means a demand. Let us see how these dogmas affect our relationships. If I come to you with a demand over you, and you do not meet my demand, then we cannot be properly related to each other. The person who lives with a dogmatic husband or wife will find that ordinances and dogmas breed bad feelings. Where do our bad feelings come from? Where do our reactions come from? Why are we living in reactions all the time? They are coming from the inner dogmas and standards that we have in our mind. These inner demands and the reactions they produce are interfering in our relationships with one another. They bring in fear — "You need to measure up. You need to live this way." If I have an "ideal wife" concept, I will bring fear and torment, not love, into our relationship. This is what will be between us because of so many dogmas.

But on the cross, the Lord destroyed all the dogmas. He destroyed the ordinances, and by that, killed the enmity. By doing away with the ordinances, the hostile feelings are automatically eliminated. So if we are related to one another not in a dogmatic way, but in a God-loving way, we are relational — forgiving, considerate, forbearing, receiving. Love is coming out. We love because He first loved us. Because we are in this vertical relationship, we cannot help but love. There is a necessity in us to receive and love others the way He loves us.

The problem many times is that we are trying to work out a horizontal relationship when we ourselves do not know the love God has toward us. We need to enjoy that unconditional love which is based on Calvary — on the precious blood, cleansing, and forgiveness. While we were yet sinners, Christ died for us; and that love is poured out in our hearts through the Holy Spirit. It is out of this love that we have love with which to love others. May the Lord show us this kind of relationship that is in the unconditional love of God. It is by our experiencing His life — by fellowshipping with Him and obeying Him — that the reality of that life will come out in perfect love which casts out all fear and brings in another kind of atmosphere.

If you will bring to your marriage relationship the unconditional love of God and not your expectancies, your standards — what you hope she will be or he will be — then you will not be disappointed. You will also avoid hurt feelings, lack of communication, and just trying to get along. None of this will come into your relationship. But if instead you have a lot of standards and expectancies and disappointed dreams, your relationship will eventually fall apart because you brought the wrong thing into it. Bring perfect love. Bring the enjoyment that you are having in fellowship with the Lord and in following Him day by day. Bring that to your relationship. And then there will be compassion, tenderheartedness, forgiveness, mercy, and enjoying God together.

It is the same with the church. If we bring views, we will be divided within a short time. But if we bring the love of God, we will have the building in love. Let us just wait before the

Lord and let Him use this word to talk to us and to purify us. Simply tell Him, "Lord, we repent for bringing so many other things to our relationships besides Your love. We want to bring Your love. So we tell You, Lord, we want to fellowship, and we want to take a step of obedience, and we want to follow You." This is the way God's love will be perfected in us.

9

The Love Life of the Bride

The Concentration of the Love Life

Embodied in the Son
— Matt. 3:17; Eph. 1:6; Col. 1:13

Our affectionate relationship as the bride to the Bridegroom is embodied in Christ! So do not bother looking at *your* love. Look at the *embodiment of love* — look at Jesus! Matthew 3:17 says, "And suddenly a voice came from heaven, saying, This is My beloved Son, in whom I am well pleased." The word *beloved* in the New Testament always refers to the object of another's love. Thus, in this verse from Matthew, "beloved" refers to Christ as the object of the Father's love. Likewise, when we are called "beloved," it is actually an identification of us as individual objects of the love of God (cf. Rom. 1:7; Col. 3:12). We are the loved ones. We are the beloved.

We need this kind of blessed detachment. Forget completely about yourself and your condition. Do not look at yourself or think about whether *you* have any potential in yourself to love the Lord affectionately as your first love. Forget about yourself altogether. What you have to see is that the unique embodiment of this love-life is in the Son. The foremost thing we need to see is that the love-life of the bride is entirely concentrated and embodied in the Son.

Ephesians 1:6 says, "To the praise of the glory of His grace, with which He graced us in the Beloved." In the Gospels the word "beloved" is used mainly as an adjective. But here in Ephesians, "Beloved" is not an adjective, but a participle (a verbal adjective). A participle is an action word, indicating that something is happening. This participle is in the perfect tense, describing a state that began to exist in the past, that exists in the present, and that will continue to exist in the future. Thus, when Ephesians 1:6 declares that we have been graced in *the Beloved,* it refers to Christ in a state of actively being loved by the Father. In other words, this love is not a static kind of love, motionless and unmoving. It is dynamic. It is constant. It is going on all the time. It never ceases. It is a radiating love that is in the Father all the time, just beaming out. When Paul says that we are graced in *"the Beloved,"* he is speaking of Christ as the present, living concentration and embodiment of the divine love. He is describing Him as continuously and perpetually being the object of the Father's love. There is a love-flow going on all the time between the Father and the Son, and we have been escorted by grace into this flow.

Colossians 1:13 says, "He has delivered us out of the authority of darkness and transferred us into the kingdom of the Son of His love." In this verse we see again how love is focused and concentrated in the Son. The Lord is identified as "the Son of His love," and we ourselves have been transferred into "the kingdom of the Son of His love." Thus, in talking about the love-life of the bride, the first thing in our consideration is *not* ourselves, but it is to see *where* this love-life is concentrated. It is concentrated and embodied in His Son. Our gaze is upon Him.

Existing in the Son — John 1:18

The second point concerning the concentration of the love-life of the bride is that it is presently existing in the Son. John 1:18 says, "No one has seen God at any time. The only begotten Son, who is into the bosom of the Father, He has declared Him." The Greek preposition here is not *in* but *into*. Thus, it is more accurately translated "*into* the bosom of the Father," rather than "*in* the bosom of the Father."

In his *Commentary on the Gospel of John,* Frederick Godet talks about the love relationship existing between the Father and the Son in John 1:18. Contrasting the prepositions *in* and *into,* he says,

"This present participle, *Who is,* refers to the permanent relation of the Son to the Father through all the stages of His divine, human, and divine-human existence. He ever presses anew with an equal intimacy into the bosom of the Father, who reveals Himself to Him in a manner suitable to His position and His work at every moment. The [Greek] form '*into* the bosom,' instead of '*in* the bosom' (the preposition of motion, instead of that of rest), expresses precisely this active and living relation. The bosom of the Father is not a place, but a life; one is *there* only in virtue of a continual moral act."

The indication here is that there is a continuous intimate love relationship going on between the Father and the Son. He is ever *into* the bosom of the Father. May God grant that *this* love-life would become our portion and our experience in the middle of our weakness so that instead of being *into* our depression, we would constantly be *into* the bosom. We would not be into our bad and unworthy feelings that cause morbid introspection, but we would be *into* a love-life that nourishes and cherishes us in our weaknesses.

In eternity past — John 17:24

The apostle John speaks of the Lord Jesus in John 13:1: "Having loved His own who were in the world, He loved them to the end." The statement "He loved them to the end" reveals that we do not possess a temporary love but a kind of love that loves us to the end or to the uttermost. This love has its roots in eternity past according to John 17:24 and Jeremiah 31:3. It is the eternal love proceeding from the eternal life of God. From eternity past to eternity future, throughout time with all its battles and problems, this love-life remains constant. This means that nothing — neither sin, the flesh, the world, the devil, distresses, or human weakness — can separate us from that love (Rom. 8:35-39). It is this love-life existing in the Son that we are called to partake of and constantly abide in.

In His earthly life — John 15:9-10

We have seen the love-life of the Lord Jesus with the Father in eternity past. Also, when He was on earth, the Lord was abiding in the Father's love. In John 15:9-10 He says, [9] "As the Father loved Me, I also have loved you; abide in My love. [10] If you keep My commandments, you will abide in My love, just as I have kept My Father's commandments and abide in His love." Here we see that the Lord's entire earthly life was lived out in the unalterable atmosphere of the Father's love.

In His heavenly life — John 4:16-17

First John 4:17 says, "As He is, so are we in this world." The context of this verse indicates that at this very moment on the throne, in the heavenly life between the Father and the Son, there exists a continuous motion of love. The Son is in a wonderful, constant love relationship with the Father. This is the meaning of the phrase "as He is." He is always and ever being loved by the Father. In the same way that the Father is presently loving the Son on the throne, He is loving us in this world. This is the meaning of the next phrase, "so are we in this world." The intensity of love that the Father has toward the Son is the same intensity that He has toward us, because we are in His Son, and His Son is in us.

The Son is not the only beloved one. We are also beloved in Him. We too are the objects of the Father's love. It is so important that we see how this love is concentrated in His Son. It was concentrated in Him during His earthly life. It is concentrated in Him now in His heavenly life. And it is concentrated in us by virtue of His indwelling life. Because of our union with Him, as He is loved, so are we loved. He cannot be loved without us getting the benefit.

In eternity future — John 17:4-5, 23-24

In John 17:4-5 the Lord prays, [4] "I have glorified You on the earth. I have finished the work which You have given Me to do. [5] And now, O Father, glorify Me together with Yourself, with the glory which I had with You before the world was." These precious words imply that in eternity future the Son will be restored to the state in which He existed in eternity past. And again in John 17:24 the Lord says, "Father, I desire that they also whom You gave Me may *be with Me where I am,* that they may behold My glory which You have given Me; for You loved Me before the foundation of the world." This request to the Father also shows us how this love-life is concentrated in the Son. We all need to be touched with the realization that the love-life of the church, His bride, is nothing less than a participation in the very love that is concentrated in the beloved Son.

Available in the Son — John 17:26; 1 John 4:15-16

This precious love-life is now available to us in the Son. In John 17:26 the Lord prays, "And I have declared to them Your name, and will declare it, that the love with which You loved Me may be in them, and I in them." Let me emphasize the last part of this verse: "That the love with which You loved Me —

that *that love* — may be *in them, and I in them.*" This is the secret! The love *in them* is equivalent to *I in them.* Notice, to be *in them* means that the love is in us, existing in our being. So the love-life of the bride is both concentrated in the Son and available to us in the Son.

First John 4:15-16 says, [15] "Whoever confesses that Jesus is the Son of God, God abides in him, and he in God. [16] And we have known and have believed *the love that God has in us.* God is love, and he who abides in love abides in God, and God in him.*" In verse 16 what John is conveying by using two perfect tenses *(have known* and *have believed)* is that we know and continue to know, and we believe and continue to believe, the love which God has *in* us. It is a love apart from ourselves. This love is a gift. This love is God's Son. This love is a love-life that is installed right into our being. We need to realize that there is not only a well of living water in us but also a well of love. There is a well of love-life, and this love-life is available in the Son.

We do not know the love which God has in us until we begin to tap into it a little bit. Then we discover there is a flow of love in our spirit and in our heart, loving and praising Him. We do not have a straitjacket religion. No! We possess a love relationship that is not only available to us but that is also waiting to be enjoyed by us!

Only one love

There is only *one* love in this universe. It is not *your* love, *his* love, *their* love, or *my* love. It is the love of the Son for the

Father, and the love of the Father for the Son, in the current of the Spirit! In the Godhead there is one reality of love flowing, and that one love is poured out into our hearts! We love with *that* love. This means that everyone is equal. No one is left out. So none of us have to look at ourselves — at our own potential and ability to love — because it is all a matter of receiving Jesus Christ, who is the concentration of the love of God. It is having this Person live in you, crying, "Abba, Father." Galatians 4:6 states it clearly: "God has sent forth the Spirit of His Son into our hearts, crying out, Abba, Father!"

There is only one love, and that love is *in* us. This relieves us from all the strain and struggle with the inner turmoils that we may go through. We say to ourselves, "I just don't have any love toward the Lord. I don't love the Lord that much." The more we say this to ourselves, the worse we feel and the more we are in the pit of despair. But, oh, that we would begin to recognize the love dwelling in us. There *is* a love in our heart — the very love of the Son of God.

The Dispensing of the Love Life

Based on redemption and receiving "the sonship" —
Gal. 4:4-6; Rom. 8:15-16

We have seen that the love-life of the bride is *concentrated* in the person of God's Son. Now we need to see the *dispensing* of the love-life. In Galatians 4:4-6 Paul shows us that this dispensing is fully based upon redemption and receiving the sonship. In verses 4-5 Paul says, [4]"But when the fullness of the time had come, God sent forth His Son, born of a woman, born under the law, [5] to redeem those who were under the law, that we might receive the sonship." To receive the *sonship* is to receive the love-life of the Son and the Father. We have been redeemed that we might receive the sonship. Then verse 6 says, "And because you are sons, God has sent forth the Spirit of His Son into our hearts, crying out, Abba, Father!" What is Paul talking about here? He is describing the dispensing of the love-life. To cry "Abba" is to participate in the intimacy between the Lord Jesus and the Father. That intimacy has been dispensed into our hearts.

The love-life is concentrated in the Son. Just stand back to behold and admire it in Him. It is thoroughly wrought in Him from eternity past to eternity future. But even more glorious is that the love-life concentrated in the Son is now dispensed into our hearts. Praise the Lord!

The nature of God's love
poured out in our hearts — Rom. 5:5

Paul declares in Romans 5:5, "Now hope does not put to shame, because the love of God has been *poured out in our hearts* through the Holy Spirit who has been given to us." This verse tells us the love of God is a dispensed thing. It is not a worked-up thing. We do not try to find it in ourselves. The love of God is a poured-out reality.

What is the nature of the experience of God's love in our hearts on a daily basis? How does it feel to have the love of God poured out in our hearts? To appreciate the nature of this poured-out love and what it is like to enjoy the Lord according to this love-life, we need to read the context of Romans 5:5. Verse 6 says, "For *while* we were yet weak." This is the condition on which the love is poured out — not when we are strong, but while we are yet weak. Note the second part of this verse: "in due time Christ died for the ungodly." If you are ungodly, you are a prime candidate for the love of God. Maybe you are thinking miserable things about yourself — that you hate yourself for the things you have done. You wish you had not done them, but you did. You did some ungodly things that you would not want anyone to know about, and you hate yourself for it. But listen to what this verse says: "Christ died for the ungodly." You are the very kind of person He shed His blood for. Despite what you have done, He loves you! This shows us the nature of the poured-out love in our hearts.

Paul further characterizes the nature of the poured-out love of God in Romans 5:7: "For scarcely for a righteous man will one die; yet perhaps for a good man someone would even dare to die." It is possible that someone might lay down his life for a righteous man. It is even imaginable that someone would die for a good man — for a person who is considered respectable and successful. We also may hear of a mother giving up her life for her own child. We can understand these kinds of love. But the love of God is altogether in another realm. Listen to what Romans 5:8 says: "But God demonstrates His own love to us, in that while we were yet sinners, Christ died for us." Once again we see the nature of the love of God: "*While* we were yet sinners." Notice the little "yets" in these verses — *yet* weak, *yet* sinners. And then in verse 10, this love goes even further: "*while* we were enemies we were reconciled to God through the death of His Son." If we thoroughly saturate ourselves with these verses, we will realize that the love of God poured out in our hearts is not a conditional love. It has nothing to do with our righteousness or whether or not we are good. It is in our weakness as sinners that the love of God is still our portion in our hearts.

Enjoyed in the fellowship of the Holy Spirit —
2 Cor. 13:14; Jude 20-21

This love-life poured out in our hearts is enjoyed by us in the fellowship of the Holy Spirit. Second Corinthians 13:14 says, "The grace of the Lord Jesus Christ, and the love of God, and the fellowship of the Holy Spirit be with you all." Here we can see that the dispensing of this love-life is in the fellowship of the Holy Spirit. The love of God with the grace of Christ is transmitted and carried into our experience and affections when we are in the fellowship of the Holy Spirit.

Jude 20-21, two of the most practical verses in the Bible, tell us how to have the fellowship of the Holy Spirit: [20] "But you, beloved, building yourselves up in your most holy faith, *praying in the Holy Spirit,* [21] *keep yourselves in the love of God,* awaiting the mercy of our Lord Jesus Christ unto eternal life." When we pray in the Holy Spirit — whether in the prayer meetings or by ourselves — we are keeping ourselves in the love of God.

Have you ever wondered what it means when someone says, "I just had to get to the prayer meeting"? In order to explain, let me use myself as an example. There are times when I really do not know how I feel about myself until I get into God's feeling about me. Often I do not know how to interpret myself. I might be depressed when God is not depressed at all. I might be in a realm that God is definitely not in. That is when I say, "I just have to get to the meeting," because it is in the meeting that we pray and keep ourselves in the love of God. In other words, we touch our spirit and enjoy the love of God resident within us.

Things are never as bad as we think they are. It is the devil that tells us all the negative things about ourselves. He is the accuser of the brethren. He is a destroyer. He is a killer. He is a cheater. He is a usurper. He is a liar. We believe lies about ourselves. But God surely does not feel that way about us. If we will just pray in the Holy Spirit, open our mouths and call on the Lord, and sing with our hearts to the Lord, we will discover that God's love *in us* is what is real.

We can keep ourselves in the love of God by praying in the Holy Spirit. The Holy Spirit is within us. The love of God and the grace of Christ will flow in us in the fellowship of the Holy Spirit. And that fellowship of the Holy Spirit is ours simply by praying in the Holy Spirit. This is how we keep ourselves in the love of God. Oh, what a love-life! This is an encouragement to everyone. Even if you feel like the most pitiful person, you are a candidate for the dispensing of this love-life. Just let the Lord in. And then keep letting Him in. Pray in the Holy Spirit and you will discover how you feel about yourself from God's point of view. You will say, "I am really in a wonderful condition! God loves me!"

Brothers and sisters, the essence of the love-life of the bride is in the enjoyment of this poured-out love-life. "The love of God has been poured out in our hearts through the Holy Spirit who was given to us" (Rom. 5:5). This love-life is concentrated in the Son, dispensed in the Holy Spirit, and enjoyed in our spirit as we pray and sing and call upon His name. This is what changes our affections.

Giving voice to it

We can pray in the Holy Spirit and keep ourselves in the love of God. The love of God is now in the Holy Spirit. It is concentrated there. The Lord Himself is the Spirit (2 Cor. 3:17-18), and this love concentrated in the Son is now dispensed into us, that is, poured out into us, through the Holy Spirit. So when we speak about the love-life of the bride, we are not speaking about fleshly energy that tries to work up a love for God. We are talking about relaxing and resting in a poured-out love that already exists in our spirit and heart. All we have to do is give voice to it. Just give voice to it a little bit. Echo it. Praise in His praising! Sing in His singing! Love in His loving!

Galatians 4:6 says, "God has sent forth the Spirit of *His Son* into our hearts, *crying out*, Abba, Father!" This seems somewhat objective — the Son is crying, "Abba, Father," in our hearts. From this verse we may think that we could put a stethoscope up to our heart and listen for an "Abba, Father" in there. But Romans 8:15 says, "You received a spirit of sonship in which *we cry out*, Abba, Father." This verse shows us that the crying is more subjective in our experience.

Who is crying "Abba, Father"? The Son in our hearts or we in our spirit? By putting these two verses together, we can see that there are not two cryings but one, and there are not two lovings but one. He cries in our crying. He loves in our loving. In our crying, it is Him — it is Him loving, worshiping, and crying "Abba." By this we can see that there is one love, and this one marvelous love poured out in our hearts is what we are giving voice to.

John 17:26 also reveals this one love. The Lord said to the Father, "And I have declared to them Your name, and will declare it, that *the love with which You loved Me may be in them, and I in them*." "The love with which You loved Me" is the *one love* — the Father's love for the Son. Then the Lord says that this love "may be in them, and I in them." That is the same *one love* now located within us. So we are talking about one love that we give voice to.

The affections of the bride

The primary way the bride is prepared is by allowing the love-life of the Father and the Son to so enter her affections that her heart is saying, "Come, Lord Jesus!" In Revelation 22:17 the Spirit and the bride say, "Come!" They say it in concert. It is not the Spirit saying "Come!" and the bride separately saying "Come!" There is only one speaking. This one speaking comes from the Spirit so saturating the bride that the bride's speaking is the Spirit's speaking. The Spirit's speaking is embodied in the bride. This shows us that the bride's readiness for the Lord's coming back is in the area of her heart and affections.

According to the last chapter of the Bible, there are genuine lovers of Jesus on the earth at the end of the age, saying, "Come, Lord Jesus!" That is, in the midst of a lawless age the bride is prepared, possessing and cultivating an affectionate relationship with the Lord. Thus, what is primary to the Lord for His coming back is not the rebuilding of the temple, the regathering of Israel, or the appearance of the Antichrist, but the love-life of His bride.

There is no higher preparation of the bride than to have her affections thoroughly wrought with the first and great commandment — "You shall *love* the LORD your God with all your heart, with all your soul, with all your mind, and with all your strength." And the second commandment is like it: "You shall *love* your neighbor as yourself" (Mark 12:30-31). Here in these verses the primary feature existing toward God and man is love — vertical love and horizontal love. By these great commandments we see that the bride will fully embody and express God's unconditional love.

The most encouraging thing is to see the source of the bride's transformed affections. These affections are existing and concentrated in God's Son, their source. That is, the love with which we love the Lord is not our own love in the sense that it originates from us. It is demonstrated, manifested, and lived out first in the Person of the Son. This means that before we measure our love for the Lord, we need to put ourselves completely aside, not considering our ability or potential to love, or even our desire to love Him. We just need to take a look at the love-life of the Lord Jesus. Look at His love for the Father. Behold how love is concentrated in Him. He is the Beloved! He is the One who abides in the Father's love. All that love is, is embodied in Him. Love exists in Him. He is the one unique concentration of divine love, and we are in this "Beloved One" as the objects of God's unconditional love.

What is the love-life of the bride? It is a love-*life* that we are talking about, not love-*behavior*. It is not that we try to love or to be loving. We are talking about a love-*life*, a life that has all the necessary affections and love already in it. It is a love that is already furnished and existing and ready to be supplied to us.

The final utterance of the Bible in Revelation 22:17 is simply, "And let him who thirsts come. And whoever wills, let him take the water of life freely." This final word of the Bible catches our attention — just come and drink the life of God freely! The truth in this verse reveals that the way the bride became the bride — with all her affections full of love for the Lord — was by drinking God as the water of life. This means an intimate love relationship with the Lord is to be found *in* the water! Drink the water of life because this water has in it the love we need to be the bride. By drinking the water of life we will become increasingly affectionate in our heart toward the Lord to become His loving bride.

SCRIPTURE INDEX

MINISTRY PUBLICATIONS

Other Available Books:

by Bill Freeman

The Supplied Life
A Daily Devotional • 409 pages

The Cross and the Self
Describes the depths of the self-life while at the same
time showing God's way of dealing with it • 321 pages

Spending Time with the Lord
A book on the practical way the Lord has preeminince in
our lives — spending quality time with Him • 224 pages

The Kingdom Life
A study in the book of James showing the nature
of the kingdom life in our daily life • 227 pages

How They Found Christ — in their own words
The personal testimonies of Augustine, Luther, Calvin, Bunyan,
Guyon, Wesley, Edwards, Whitefield, Finney, Müller, Murray,
H. W. Smith, H. Taylor, Spurgeon, A. B. Simpson, and W. Nee
Edited by Bill Freeman • 201 pages

Our Common Oneness

A study in the book of Romans revealing the common
oneness of all believers regardless of backgrounds • 284 pages

Calling Upon the Name of the Lord

A study of the meaning, history, and basis of
calling upon the Name of the Lord • 149 pages

Seeing and Feeling the Church

A study of Paul's prayers in the book of Ephesians • 138 pages

The Triune God in Experience

A study of the experiential emphasis on the
Triune God throughout church history • 391 pages

Ordering Information:

You may use any of the following ways to order books from *Ministry Publications:*

(1) Available at Christian bookstores everywhere through
    Spring Arbor Distributors and *Anchor Distributors*
(2) Write: P. O. Box 12222, Scottsdale, AZ 85267 • USA
(3) Phone: (480) 948-4050 / (800) 573-4105
(4) Fax: (480) 922-1338
(5) E-mail: MinWord12@aol.com
(6) Web site: http://www.thechristian.org
(7) Amazon.com / barnesandnoble.com